The *Things To Do With Your Computer* series has been prepared for Signet by dilithium Press, a renowned publisher of high-quality, easy-to-understand, technically accurate computer books. No matter what personal computer you use, Signet dilithium has a book for you.

THINGS TO DO WITH YOUR TI-99/4A COMPUTER

THINGS TO DO WITH YOUR COMMODORE® 64™ COMPUTER

THINGS TO DO WITH YOUR COMMODORE® VIC 20™ COMPUTER

THINGS TO DO WITH YOUR TRS-80® MODEL 4 COMPUTER

THINGS TO DO WITH YOUR TRS-80® MODEL 100 COMPUTER

THINGS TO DO WITH YOUR APPLE® COMPUTER

THINGS TO DO WITH YOUR IBM® PERSONAL COMPUTER

THINGS TO DO WITH YOUR ATARI® COMPUTER

THINGS TO DO WITH YOUR OSBORNE® COMPUTER

THINGS TO DO WITH YOUR TRS-80® COLOR COMPUTER

THINGS TO DO WITH YOUR APPLE® COMPUTER

by

Jerry Willis

Merl Miller

Nancy Morrice

A SIGNET BOOK

NEW AMERICAN LIBRARY

TIMES MIRROR

NAL BOOKS ARE AVAILABLE AT QUANTITY DISCOUNTS
WHEN USED TO PROMOTE PRODUCTS OR SERVICES.
FOR INFORMATION PLEASE WRITE TO PREMIUM MARKETING DIVISION,
THE NEW AMERICAN LIBRARY, INC., 1633 BROADWAY,
NEW YORK, NEW YORK 10019.

TRADEMARK ACKNOWLEDGMENTS

Apple, Apple Computer, Inc.; Apple Silentype Printer, Apple Computer, Inc.; Bank Street Writer, Broderbund Software; CAT Modem, Novation; Cdex, Cdex Corporation; Choplifter, Broderbund Software; CompuServe, CompuServe, Inc.; CP/M, Digital Research; dBase II, Ashton Tate, Inc.; Deadline, Infocom; DEFENDER, Williams Electronics, Inc.; DIALOG, DIALOG Information Services, Inc.; Dow Jones News/Retrieval, Dow Jones & Company, Inc.; The Einstein Compiler, Einstein Corp.; Gorgon, Sirius Software; HIPAD DIGITIZER, Houston Instrument; IBM Selectric, International Business Machines; Magic Memory, ARTSCI, Inc.; Money Street, Bullseye Software; PAC-MAN, Bally Midway Mfg. Co.; SAT Exam Prep Series, Krell Software; Smith-Corona TP-1, Smith-Corona, Inc.; The Source, Source Telecomputing; Suspended, Infocom; UCSD Pascal, Regents of the University of California, San Diego; VIS\BRIDGE/DJ, Solution, Inc.; VisiCalc, VisiCorp; VIZ-A-CON, Abacus Associates; Voyage of the Valkyrie, Advanced Operating Systems; Zork I, II, III, Infocom

PHOTOGRAPH ACKNOWLEDGMENTS

Figures 1.1, 1.2, 1.3, 1.4, 4.1, 10.1, 10.2, 10.3, 10.4 and 10.5
courtesy of Apple Computer, Inc.
Figures 2.1 and 7.1 courtesy of Broderbund Software.
Figure 2.2 courtesy of Sirius Software.
Figure 2.3 courtesy of Advanced Operating Systems.
Figures 2.4, 2.5, 2.6, 2.7, 2.8, 2.9 and 2.10 courtesy of Infocom.
Figure 2.11 courtesy of Mind Systems Corporation.
Figure 2.12 courtesy of Quality Softwear.
Figures 3.1 and 3.2 courtesy of ALF Products, Inc.
Figure 3.3 courtesy of Syntauri corporation.
Figure 3.4 courtesy of Houston Instruments.
Figure 3.5 courtesy of Versa Computing, Inc.
Figure 4.3, 4.4 and 4.5 courtesy of Developmental Learning Materials.
Figure 4.6 courtesy of Lightning Software, Inc.
Figure 4.7 courtesy of Academic Hallmarks.
Figures 4.8, 4.9 and 4.10 courtesy of Computer Advanced Ideas.
Figure 4.11 courtesy of Sunburst Communications, Inc.
Figures 5.1 and 5.2 courtesy of Proforma Software.

SIGNET, SIGNET CLASSIC, MENTOR, PLUME, MERIDIAN and NAL BOOKS
are published by the The New American Library, Inc.,
1633 Broadway, New York, New York 10019

First Printing, November, 1983

1 2 3 4 5 6 7 8 9

PRINTED IN THE UNITED STATES OF AMERICA

This book is the result of the creative efforts and research talent of the editorial staff at dilithium Press. The authors gratefully acknowledge the work of the staff and would like to publicly recognize each of the people who contributed to the creation of this book:

Nancy Morrice, *Senior Editor*

Deborrah Willis, *Editor*

Cleborne D. Maddux, *Technical Writer*

D. LaMont Johnson, *Technical Writer*

Jane Sterrett

Ann L. Hovland

Jo Anne Gilbert

Erin Lommen

Tamera Alen

Contents

CHAPTER ONE

Introducing the Apple

Although ads, articles, and books about personal computers seem to be everywhere today, the plain fact is that most of us were not prepared for the *computer revolution*. We attended schools that had no courses on computers, and we took jobs that did not require us to deal with them. Things have changed quickly, however. Computers are on many Christmas lists today, because many of the models play great video games. They are more and more common in the nation's classrooms, and an increasing number of professional and technical workers use computers in their jobs. The computer is a versatile machine that can do many different jobs and provide hours of recreational enjoyment.

You can use your computer to help with personal finances, to play games, or to help your children learn. (We have yet to find a computer that can bring us a beer during the ball game, but at the rate new things happen in the computer industry, one may be just around the corner.)

Figure 1.1 Professional workers using an Apple computer on the job

Figure 1.2 Young people working with computers in the classroom

Figure 1.3 Enjoying an Apple Computer at home

This book tells you about many of the useful things a computer can do. It was written specifically for people who own or are considering the purchase of an Apple computer. It may also help you decide if you really want to buy a computer. This is one in a series of books on popular computer models. If you are shopping for a computer, you may want to read more than one book, so you can compare the features and characteristics of several different models. This information will help you select the best computer for your needs.

Actually, the computer is just like any other machine or tool. The person using it determines how it is used and its power. Contrary to popular belief, computers really aren't intelligent machines that can take the place of humans. There is no more chance that computers will take over than there is that washing machines will rule the world. The worst that could happen is you may waste some of your time or money if you use the computer unwisely. That doesn't mean every owner learns the same things and uses the computer in the same way.

You can use your computer on many different levels. You may choose to regard your computer as you do any other appliance and simply use it as a labor-saving device. Or you may become fascinated with its internal workings and continue studying and learning about computers for the rest of your life.

This introductory book is intended to help you use a computer as an appliance. The good news is that you aren't going to have to learn much about hardware, software, bits, bytes, ROMs, RAMs, and other computer things. The bad news is that you will have to learn a little jargon. You had to know a little jargon to learn to drive your car. Most of us learned the terms, concepts, and principles needed to drive a car as we were growing up. By the time we were teenagers the automobile had become a commonplace necessity for most families. Common terms such as ignition, premium gas, gas pedal and brake were jargon when the automobile was first introduced. Today we take these terms for granted. Jargon associated with the use of telephones has also become a part of our everyday language. The same thing will be true with computers. The next generation may well take a computer on the dining table or in the recreation room for granted. Kids will take terms like RAM and ROM in stride because they grew up with them and understand how to use computers. Unfortunately we are part of a transitional generation. We didn't grow up with this inexpensive and useful technology. We are *automobile literate* and *telephone literate*, but we aren't *computer literate*. We'll try to help you solve this problem in three ways. First, as we introduce each computer term, we define it. Second, we have a little introduction to computer terms later on in this chapter. It's not a glossary but will give you some background. Third, there is a glossary in the back of the book.

Figure 1.4 The Apple IIe personal computer with a video monitor and single disk drive

HARDWARE AND SOFTWARE

Before we get into specifics, it is important that you understand two general computer terms. *Hardware* may conjure up visions of eggbeaters or pipe fittings, but it really refers to any piece of computer equipment. The computer itself is a piece of hardware, and so are other accessories like printers and disk drives (See Chapter Ten).

Software refers to the programs that make your computer do a specific task. The media often make it seem very easy to make a computer do what you want it to. Television programs and movies often show people making a computer perform simply by talking to it. As you may have already discovered, your computer isn't that friendly yet. (Actually, we talk to our computers all the time, usually when they don't do what we want, and what we say is often x-rated!). Communicating with a computer today usually involves typing instructions on its keyboard or transferring information stored electronically on a *cassette* or *disk* into the electronic memory of the computer. The instructions a computer follows when it performs a particular task are called *software*. It takes software to make hardware useful.

A comparison of stereo equipment and records may make the relationship between hardware and software a little clearer. The computer itself is a piece of hardware and is like a stereo. By itself, the stereo cannot create music. The computer can't do anything by itself, either. A computer program is like a cassette or record containing music. When the cassette is put in the stereo, the usefulness of the stereo becomes obvious. When a program is put into a computer, the computer also begins to be useful. Just as your stereo will play hard rock, Italian opera, or country music, your computer can play a video game, help you learn a new language, or balance your checkbook. Just insert the correct program (or software).

The comparison stops there. A stereo with a cassette deck will play most of the commercially available cassettes, but computer programs are written for specific computer systems. A program written for the Radio Shack computer, for example, cannot be used without modification on your Apple computer. Shopping for computer software is more difficult than shopping for a new music cassette, because software is developed for specific computers.

DO YOU HAVE TO LEARN TO PROGRAM YOUR COMPUTER?

You may have heard that you will have to learn to *program* the computer before it will do anything useful. It is true your computer can't do anything until it gets a program written in a computer language it understands, but *you* don't have to write it.

Computer languages can take weeks or months to learn. Programs (software) that do complicated and useful things take time to write. Writing computer programs is an interesting hobby (or profession) that thousands of people enjoy. You may decide that you want to learn to write programs in a language like BASIC (Beginners All-purpose Symbolic Instruction Code). (We'll talk more about BASIC and other computer languages in Chapter Nine.) Programming doesn't appeal to everyone who uses a computer, however. Fewer than ten percent of the people who own small or personal computers spend much of their time writing programs. This means the great majority of people do not write their own software. Instead, they buy software someone else has written. That's what we discuss in this book: ready-made software for the Apple II, II+, and IIe computers. We'll tell you about software that lets the computer do hundreds of things, where to get the software, and the strengths and weaknesses we see in the software.

OH, NO! JARGON!

It's not as bad as all that. We're just going to give you a little guided tour of jargon. The Apple IIe computer is made up of one main component that houses the keyboard and the main circuit board. On the back of this unit are several plugs that let you connect the Apple to other pieces of hardware, such as disk drives and a printer. These are called *I/O ports*. I/O is short for *input/output*. Ports let the computer bring data in for processing and out to other peripherals. The Apple IIe also has a set of *expansion slots* on its main circuit board where accessories can be installed. For example, you can add any of several types of optional I/O ports to the computer by inserting it into one of the expansion slots. Many other types of accessories are also added through the slots.

One item you must have to use the computer is some form

of *video display*. The video display is often your TV set, but it can also be a piece of hardware called a *monitor*.

All this hardware is important. It's nothing, however, without software. Software is the instructions the computer follows to do something. As we mentioned earlier, a set of instructions that tell the computer to perform a particular task such as play a game or teach long division is called a *program*. You can either buy programs written by someone else (*canned software*) or you can write them yourself. If you write your own programs, you are *programming* the computer. There are thousands of canned programs for the Apple computer.

No matter where you get the programs, you will need to store them somewhere when they are not in use. When you want the computer to follow the instructions in a particular piece of software, you tell the computer to load that program into its memory. If the program is stored on a cassette tape, the computer can read the electronic codes stored on the tape and copy those codes into its electronic *memory*. If it is on a disk, the computer will read the codes stored on the magnetic surface of the disk. When the computer is told to *execute* or *run* a program, it looks at the codes in its memory and does whatever those codes tell it to do. The memory where the codes for your cassette program is stored is called *RAM*, for *random access memory*. It can be used for storing programs, as well as any data the computer may need (for example, your name, your answer to a math problem, or the number of blue widgets in inventory). Another type of memory is called *ROM*. ROM is short for *read only memory*. This type of memory has instructions in it that were installed at the factory and cannot be changed. The Apple IIe has enough ROM to store just over 16,000 characters. The instructions in ROM control the computer. The Apple computer can *read* the instructions stored in the ROM.

Each unit of memory large enough to hold the code for one character is called a *byte*. One byte of memory can hold the code for one character. One *kilobyte* is 1024 bytes, but most people just say *1K* instead of one kilobyte. That means a computer with 16K of RAM has enough memory to store 16 times 1024 (16384) characters. Some programs require a large amount of RAM when they run. A program that calls for 24K of RAM won't run on a computer with only 16K of RAM.

The last thing we'll look at and the first thing you'll usually look at when you turn your computer on is the *video screen*. The screen is sometimes called the *CRT* (for cathode ray tube) or the *video display*. As you type letters and numbers on the keyboard, they show up on the screen. The display that's created is called an *alphanumeric display* because it is made up of letters and numbers. If your three-year-old writes on the screen with a crayon, you have a *mess*. If you give the computer instructions that direct it to draw a picture of an ocean with a ship riding at anchor on a blue-sky summer day, you have a *graphics display*. What you see on the screen is composed of special graphics characters. Very good graphics displays that show fine detail are made up of tiny dots of color called *picture elements* or *pixels*. The Apple computer can create high-quality pictures made up of thousands of tiny multicolored pixels. Graphics of this type are called *high-resolution* or *HI-RES* graphics.

These are some of the more commonly used terms and jargon associated with the Apple computer. As new words are used in the following chapters, we will try to define them the first time they are used. Remember too, that the glossary at the end of the book lists several hundred computer terms and defines them for you.

WHAT'S IN THE REST OF THIS BOOK

Before a computer balances your checkbook or helps you beat back invading hordes of space no-good-niks, you will have to learn a bit about how it works and what it can do. In addition, you will quickly discover that there are many different ways to get the computer to do a particular job. There are, for example, at least fifty good programs you can buy for the Apple that help you balance your checkbook. There are thousands of video games for the Apple, some good, a few great ones, and many that can only be described as terrible. You won't want to buy everything that is available, but how do you decide? This book should help you make good decisions. It describes many of the programs currently available for Apple computers. We assume that you aren't a computer expert but would like to know a lot more about how you can use an Apple in your office, home, or school. If you already own an Apple computer, you may learn some new ways of using it while reading the chapters that follow. Each chapter in *Things To Do With Your Apple Computer* introduces you to one area of computer application. The chapters begin with some general background information. Then detailed information on Apple programs or accessories is presented. This book won't make you a computer *expert*. Instead, it will help you become an informed consumer.

You can skip around in this book as much as you like. If you are interested in video games, for example, you don't need to read the chapter on business applications. Here is a list of the chapters and a short description of their content:

Chapter One. *Introducing the Apple*. In this chapter you find out what a personal computer is and some ways you can use it. We also give you a brief guided tour of the Apple computer and we introduce *software* and *hardware*.

Chapter Two. *Fun and Games*. This chapter describes the various recreational uses of the computer, with an emphasis on video games. It includes reviews of many of the most popular games.

Chapter Three. *Arts and Crafts*. You may not become a modern day Van Gogh or Bach, but there is more artistic potential in the computer than you might expect. It is more than a number cruncher! The Apple is a good arts and crafts computer. It has excellent color graphics and some sound capabilities, and there are some exciting music and visual arts programs.

Chapter Four. *The Apple II as Teacher*. There are two aspects of educational computing: the use of the computer to teach other academic subjects and the computer as a topic of study itself. Over a thousand programs for the Apple teach everything from grammar to algebra. In addition, many books and programs that can help you become *computer literate* on the Apple are described.

Chapter Five. *Home Finance, Record Keeping, and Health Care*. The time it takes to keep track of family finances can be cut drastically by computerizing some of these tasks. Several programs for the Apple can help you with home finance and record keeping.

Chapter Six. *Tapping into the World: Telecommunications*. Did you know the Apple sitting on your kitchen table can be used to communicate with computers all over the world? You can get all sorts of information, from Italian train schedules to reviews of the latest movies. This chapter shows you how.

Chapter Seven. *Word Processing*. This chapter explains how the Apple can be turned into a very smart electronic typewriter and word processor for home, professions and businesses. With the right programs, a good printer, a few extra pieces of hardware, and some practice, your Apple can rival word processing systems that cost four or five times as much.

Chapter Eight. *The Apple: Your Business Assistant*. This chapter is a brief overview of the ways a computer can be used on the job, concluding with a description of some of the business software available.

Chapter Nine. *Programming*. Writing instructions that tell a computer what to do is called programming, which is covered here, as well as the various languages available on the Apple (for example, BASIC, PILOT, Logo).

Chapter Ten. *Peripherals*. The final chapter deals with accessories such as disk drives, printers, extra memory, and more.

A NOTE ON THE APPLE II

We'll focus on the Apple IIe, the newest version of the Apple II computer, which had been on the market only a few months when this book was written. Most, but not all, the information is accurate for the Apple II and the Apple II+, which are older versions of the same computer system. The Apple IIe has a better keyboard, more memory, and a new method of expanding the video display to a 24-line by 80-character format.

Over ninety-five percent of the software developed for the older Apple II+ will run on the IIe. And most of the peripherals we review will work with both the IIe and older versions of the Apple II.

CHAPTER TWO

Fun And Games

OK, so you finally made the big decision. You signed your life away to the finance company and brought home your Apple IIe computer with all the accessories. You've astounded your friends (and appeased your spouse, or tried to) by demonstrating how it can analyze real estate investments, improve your child's spelling, and store your favorite recipe for chocolate-covered cabbage. That's all fine and good, but now that the friends have gone home and everyone except you is in bed, it's time to get down to business. Time to put your computer through its paces. Time for what you *really* bought your Apple for: playing computer games!

COMPUTER GAMES ARE VERY POPULAR

While it's true that computers can be useful for a rapidly growing variety of tasks in the home, it's also a fact that they are *most often* used for game-playing. That's not hard to understand when you consider the popularity of arcade games. Everywhere you go these days—grocery stores, convenience markets, restaurants, malls—you see people putting quarters in arcade game machines. You can play some of these same games at home on your Apple. Literally thousands of games have been written for the Apple!

There are several computers that can run games strikingly similar to these arcade games, and the Apple is one of them. In fact, your Apple takes a backseat to no other home computer when it comes to game playing. It displays fast-moving, high-quality color graphics on a television screen or video monitor; it has a built-in speaker for generating some passable sound effects; and it has connectors for game paddles. You can't play all the games on it that you would on an arcade machine, but that's not surprising. Arcade games cost thousands of dollars and use a screen that is custom-designed for a single use!

TYPES OF GAMES FOR THE APPLE

We will review several different types of computer games in this chapter, beginning with action games. There are also fantasy games, simulations, card games, games of chance, board games, and sports games. You may have a favorite type, but we suggest you read a few of the reviews in every category. While action games are familiar to most people, you may be surprised at how many other types of games there are for the Apple IIe.

A Word of Caution

We have not attempted to review every one of the games available today for the Apple computer. There are too many of them, and quite a few are so poor they do not deserve mention. It would take an entire book to review all the bad software. Therefore, we decided to use the space in this book to describe software we found acceptable, if not excellent. Even with that limitation, we were not able to describe all the good software that was available when this book was written. We hope this chapter will at least give you an idea of the type of recreational software you can buy for the Apple IIe.

Action Games

The most popular of all computer games are the action games. You are probably familiar with them because most arcade games are action games. There are hundreds (maybe even thousands) of action games you can play on your Apple computer. (The violence in some of these games has been criticized by people who fear that playing them could lead to increased violence in real life. That may or may not be true. We simply do not have the evidence to determine what effect playing action games might have.)

Actually, there are several subtypes of action games. The most popular type pits your spaceship/missile base/tank against hordes of attacking enemy ships/creatures/tanks. We call these *bang, bang, shoot 'em up* games. That certainly sums it up well. You spend your time zapping alien spaceships or blasting asteroids. In other types of action games, you guide race cars around a track or direct a small character around a maze while it's pursued by monsters. The strong graphics and sound capabilities of the Apple computer make it especially well-suited for action games. To play them, you need rapid responses, usually through your joystick, and good eye-hand coordination. You can learn the rules of these games quickly, but you earn high points only if you can respond quickly and accurately to changing events on the video screen.

Choplifter

Choplifter is a one-player action game available on diskette for $34.95 from Broderbund Software. The game uses advanced high-resolution graphics and realistic sound effects. It came in first in *Softalk Magazine*'s balloting for the best software released in 1982.

The setting for this unique game is the mythical Empire of Bungeling. Militant army factions there have engineered the kidnapping of sixty-four people at a United Nations meeting. The hostages are spirited away and imprisoned in four barracks near the eastern border of Bungeling.

You oppose the kidnapping and have set up a rescue command post just across the eastern border. As the game opens, you are notified that sixteen of the hostages have broken out of one of the barracks and need help desperately. You can depend only on your heavily-armed helicopter and your own flying skill to carry off the rescue.

A joystick is optional in this game, but adds realism. Your helicopter is extremely responsive to you as a pilot. You'll have to be careful or you'll crash before you even get to the hostages! You control the movement of the helicopter and its armament by pressing keys on the keyboard or with a joystick. It takes a while to get the hang of flying the thing, but with practice you can do it.

If you do manage to stay in the air and fly over the border to the area where the hostages are kept, you have to contend with enemy tanks. Fortunately, as long as you are in the air they cannot raise their guns high enough to threaten your safety. You can drop bombs on them or fire machine guns at them (you have an unending supply of ammunition) but unlike most arcade games, that won't earn you any points. The only thing that counts is rescuing the hostages. The only reason to go after a tank is to protect the hostages.

If you fly carefully and land just as carefully, the hostages will run out and jump on board your ship. If you aren't careful, you can land on top of the hostages you are trying to free, or the helicopter rotor can do them in. Of course, the tanks can shoot the hostages if you don't get there first and protect them.

Sound difficult? It is. Oh, and don't forget the jets and the smart bomb. Enemy jets attack and fire rockets at you and the hostages. If your helicopter is in the air, it can be shot down. If it's on the ground, it can be blown up, but you're a more difficult target on the ground. The smart bomb can bomb you and the hostages while you're on the ground, or it can run into you in the air.

We mentioned that you get no points for destroying enemy

Figure 2.1 Choplifter

craft. The only points come in the form of a banner on the display that is a running count of how many hostages you have returned safely to your base, how many are aboard the helicopter, and how many are still in the hands of the enemy.

Like most action games, there's a lot of violence in *Choplifter*. We may be splitting hairs, but we think the violence in this one is a shade different from what is found in many action games. The points don't come from blasting the enemy, but from saving your friends. In fact, blasting the enemy won't really get you anywhere. The only motivation for doing so at all is to protect yourself or the hostages. It's still a *shoot 'em up*, mind you, but the moral tone of this game seems a cut above many arcade-type games. Some players may not feel comfortable with *Choplifter*. Unlike most other computer games, this game is an unfunny simulation of some very serious past history.

Be that as it may, the technical quality of this game is

definitely superior. The sound effects are excellent. The graphics are some of the best you'll see in games for the Apple or for any other small computer. The only weakness seems to be the fact that once you've saved all the hostages, the game is over. You'll find yourself wishing for a way to continue.

Still, this is an excellent example of an action game. They really don't come any better. It might be best not to make this the first action game you play on an Apple. You might never be satisfied with anything less!

Raster Blaster and **Pinball Construction Set**

Raster Blaster is an excellent pinball simulation available for $29.95 from BudgeCo. The game requires 48K of RAM, and game paddles are recommended.

The graphics and sound effects are excellent in this popular game. On the left side of the video display is the image of a rather traditional-looking pinball machine. The right side shows the score, the player, and the balls remaining.

The game incorporates all the standard pinball equipment. The ball can roll through any of the four lanes at the top of the screen. There are four very sensitive bumpers in the center of play. When the ball hits these bumpers, it rebounds with realistic pinball sound effects. If you tire of the sound effects, you can have silent play by pressing the S key.

Raster Blaster includes bumpers, flippers, and targets, and has two levels of difficulty. Up to four players may participate, each with five balls.

The outstanding part of this game is the realistic ball movement. It's easy to forget that it's all electronic and that gravity really has nothing to do with the action. If you're a pinball wizard (or want to be), you'll like this game.

Pinball Construction Set is also by BudgeCo. It is for the dedicated pinball player who tires of the standard *Raster Blaster* board layout. This software comes on diskette for $39.95 and requires 48K, DOS 3.3, and a two-button joystick. This *kit* is typical of a new kind of software you can use to custom-design your own game.

When you load the program, the first thing you see is an empty pinball playing board on the left side of the screen and a large number of pinball parts, such as flippers, bumpers, and targets, on the right side. There is also a hand, which you can maneuver with the joystick. When you want the hand to stop, you return the joystick to the center position. To pick up one of the pinball parts, you use the joystick to place the hand so that the index finger is touching the part you want. You then press the joystick button and hold it down, and the hand grasps the part. You can then use the joystick to place the part wherever you want it on the playing board. And you release the button to leave the part in place.

You can use an electronic paintbrush to color the parts, a hammer to change the shape of parts, and scissors to cut knobs off. A magnifying glass makes it possible to paint very tiny parts.

After you have created a pleasing layout, you can decrease or increase gravity, speed, bumper strength, resilience of collisions, and values for score and noise. When you have designed the game, you test it, play it, and save it.

This program is the next logical step beyond *Raster Blaster*. It's creative and ensures that you'll never tire of computer pinball.

Cosmic Balance

Cosmic Balance is a design-it-yourself *shoot 'em up*. This game combines some of the strategic elements of adventure games with the fast pace of an action game. This is a good illustration of how game categories are beginning to merge. *Cosmic Balance* is available for $39.95 from Strategic Simulations Inc. You'll need 48K and a disk drive.

There are six different game plots. After you have learned the game in the first plot, you can design your own space ship or fleet of space ships. You choose what weapons to include, the size of the ship, and the field of fire each weapon covers. If you like a design, you can save it for later use.

Play in this game reminds us a little of football. The action takes place in sixteen-second bursts after you have designed your ship and made other choices related to the upcoming battle. You may play against ships designed by a human opponent or by the computer.

We could have discussed this game in the simulation category. Still, it also resembles an action game. Call it a *thinking man's shoot 'em up* if you choose. If you're looking for an action game requiring some strategy rather than simply fast reflexes, you're likely to enjoy this one.

The Video Arcade

The Video Arcade ($59.95 from Broderbund Software) is the next step beyond *Cosmic Balance*. In *Cosmic Balance* you design your own ships within a series of preset plots. In *The Video Arcade* you design your own action games.

You can draw your own geometric or free-form shapes, choose the paths they will move along, create sounds, and otherwise design your own arcade-style game. Several good sample games are included so you can see what is possible.

This program is complex but fun. We consider it part of an important trend in game software. This trend emphasizes giving the player more control of the game than ever before.

Gorgon

This section on action games wouldn't really be complete without a review of a traditional *bang, bang, shoot 'em up* of the arcade variety. *Gorgon* comes on disk for $39.95 from Sirius Software, Inc.

If you have played the popular *Defender* arcade game, then you know *Gorgon*. You are the pilot of a fighting space ship charged with protecting humans from various nasties who dive down and attempt to carry them off. You can blast the nasties with your laser before they do their dirty work or after they have seized the helpless human. If you wait until after, you must catch the human and take him safely back to the planet's surface. To help you anticipate what's coming, you have a radar screen at the top of your display. It shows you where

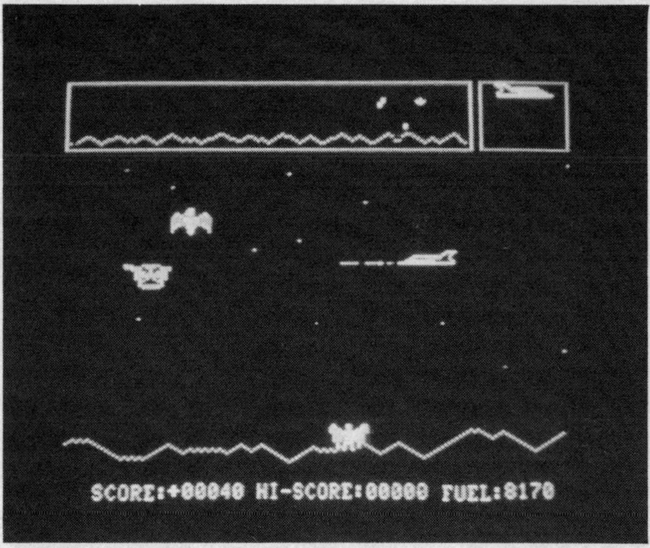

Figure 2.2 Gorgon

the nasties will be coming from. To complicate things, you can run out of fuel at any time, or you might kill the human you are trying to protect if you fly too low.

'Pillar Munch

'Pillar Munch is typical of another type of action game: *eat 'em up*! These games were inspired by the popularity of the *PAC-MAN* arcade game. There are many of these games but we chose *'Pillar Munch* for another reason. It is a "free" game written by Richard A. Nedbal and listed in *NIBBLE* magazine. There's a catch, of course. To get this game free, you'll have to type in the entire program (over 300 lines). This is time-consuming, and if you make errors, the game will not perform properly. Nevertheless, there is satisfaction in getting an enjoyable game for the price of a magazine, even if it takes some effort.

In *'Pillar Munch*, you are a caterpiller whose goal is to eat the leaves on the screen. As you eat more and more leaves, you get longer and longer. As you get longer, it becomes more difficult to maneuver around the screen. The object of the game is to continue eating leaves until you grow long enough to turn into a butterfly.

Sound easy? We forgot to mention that you must move around the display without bumping into your own growing body, bird droppings (that's right, folks, *bird droppings*!), or barriers. There are six levels of difficulty. In all but the first two levels, you can eliminate bird droppings by hitting the space bar and spitting on the droppings.

This game is fun and interesting, but it's a bit long for a type-it-yourself. If you aren't interested in typing in the program yourself, there is an alternative. Many computer magazines sell the major programs listed in each issue on cassette tapes or diskettes. Such a service is available from *NIBBLE* magazine, which is written especially for Apple computer users. Diskettes are available for $20 to $30. The disk containing *'Pillar Munch* and two other programs sells for approximately $19.95 plus shipping charges. Write for complete information. Subscriptions to the magazine itself are available for $19.95 per year.

inCider magazine is another good source of free game programs. Subscriptions are $25 per year.

Fantasy Games

Fantasy or adventure games represent an exciting departure from the typical computer game. They were probably inspired by the popular Dungeons and Dragons game, originally a loosely-structured game played entirely without a computer. The game became popular on college campuses in the late seventies and soon spread to high schools and even elementary schools.

Fantasy or adventure games usually don't depend on fast action, laser guns, or attacking space ships for their appeal. Instead, they depend on the story line. Wizards, trolls, and other magical beings are the characters in these games. They require thoughtful strategy and imaginative problem-solving, and appeal more to older children or adults.

Most of the early fantasy or adventure games were text-only, with no graphics. You actually read the entire game, selecting certain options as the game went on. Typical of this game is the popular *Adventure Series* by Adventure International, available for most microcomputers, including Apple. The series was written by Scott Adams, one of the first authors of adventure games, and includes *Pirate Adventure*, *Adventureland*, *Mystery Fun House*, and *Ghost Town*. The series is still popular and has its devoted followers. The pace of these games is so slow a complete game can take days, weeks, or even months to complete. An interesting feature of most of these games is that they can be saved on cassette or disk at any point. Later, you can enter the game where you left off.

An adventure game is likely to begin with a paragraph that sets the scene for the simulation: *You are standing on the edge of a forest. There is a narrow winding road that leads out of the forest and winds through the hills to a large stone house. The house stands on the edge of a cliff and is shrouded in fog. You see a footprint!*

All adventure simulations put you in a particular environment (forest, cave with many chambers, castle with many rooms, maze), give you a task to perform (stay alive, get out, find the treasure, rescue the prisoners), and put all sorts of dangers in your way (monsters, cliffs, sorcerers, enemy soldiers, bombs).

Two final ingredients of an adventure simulation are incomplete information and ways of getting that information. You begin the adventure without all the information you need. However, there are ways to learn more about the simulation's environment and how to deal successfully with the adventure. Most adventures require you to move about through a series of *rooms*. The term room really refers to different segments of the simulation, such as cities, chambers in a cave, and so on.

The instructions that come with most adventures strongly recommend that you make a map of your travels. Unless you have an excellent memory, it is almost impossible to master most adventures without creating a map. There are many rooms to explore and many dead ends or dangers you will want to avoid.

Adventure games let you move about the rooms by giving the computer instructions like GO AHEAD, TURN LEFT, CLIMB STAIRS, DIG OUT. Depending on the adventure, it may understand only a few instructions or several hundred. Some games even let you create your own characters and move them about the simulation. You can endow different characters with different powers and send them against foes they are likely to overcome. A sorcerer might go against a wicked magician, and a powerful Samson type might fight a giant. However, things do not always work out as you hope, and it is not unusual to lose some of your characters in the adventure.

If you like strategy, enjoy solving intricate puzzles, and have time to devote to it, playing adventure games can be a pleasant addiction.

Pirate Adventure

In *Pirate Adventure* ($19.95) you are searching for Long John Silver's treasure. The treasure is hidden somewhere on a strange island. From a flat in London, you must find your way to the island. Once you're there, you can begin using some of the items you find to help you locate the treasure. There are many dangers on the island, and you must keep your wits about you or be killed and end the game!

This is a text-only game—there are no graphics. As you move through the adventure, the computer tells you what is happening. You move about by issuing a series of two-word commands such as "GET RUM" (for *get the rum*), GO AHEAD, and LOOK UP. The computer will respond with answers such as "I see nothing of interest."

This is one of the twelve in the Scott Adams Adventure Series, which are classified into three sets, one intended for beginners, one for players with moderate skill, and one for advanced players. *Pirate Adventure* is for beginners. However, text-only adventure games require logic and patience beyond most children (and many adults). They are really not well-suited for most children younger than thirteen or so.

Voyage of the Valkyrie

Recently, another type of fantasy or adventure game has emerged. This type still relies on magic, demons, and wizards but also uses detailed graphics and may use sound. A good example of this variation is *Voyage of the Valkyrie*, available from Advanced Operating Systems on disk for $29.95. The game has some of the characteristics of classic action games and some of the characteristics of more typical fantasy games.

The object of the game is to find and capture ten castles in an imaginary kingdom called Fugloy. Finding the castles—difficult enough in itself—represents the first part of this game. Play in this portion is similar to the classic fantasy-adventure game. All sorts of perils lie in wait as you conduct your search. The game comes with over 10 pages of instructions and an

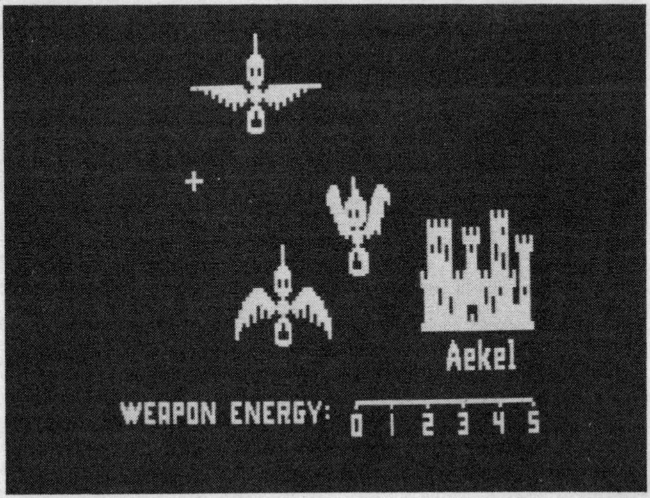

Figure 2.3 Voyage of the Valkyrie

assortment of maps of Fugloy. If you can find your way to a castle, you must attack it. The castles are defended by flocks of crazy birds that try to crash into you and stop you. You use your joystick or game paddle to center crosshairs on each one before firing. Since the castles are located on islands, you must return to your base periodically to refuel. There are ten levels of difficulty in *Voyage of the Valkyrie*. At each succeeding level, there are more birds, so you will have to use more of your fuel. If you run out of fuel over the ocean, you're a goner.

In the second part of the game, play is similar to the *bang, bang, shoot 'em up* variety of action game found in arcades. Graphics are obviously important, and they are quite good. Our only criticism is that the graphics are not in color. The excellent sound effects include music. At various points in the game, the computer plays excerpts from Wagner's *Ride of the Valkyrie*.

As we mentioned earlier, fantasy games have traditionally depended more on strategy and logic and less on fine muscle coordination and quick reactions. However, we suspect that future games will, like *Voyage of the Valkyrie*, merge some of the aspects of action games with fantasy games. Fantasy games will probably continue to appeal mostly to older children and adults, because of the logic required.

Other companies selling adventure-fantasy software for the Apple include Epyx, Quality Software, Sir-Tech Software, Synergistic Software, and Infocom Inc.

Zork I, II, and III

The *Zork* adventure games ($39.95 each) from Infocom have enjoyed fantastic popularity. They are made for several computers. Their claim to fame is the large vocabulary and complicated syntax that the program understands. The *Zork* trilogy understands complex, lengthy sentences, not just the two-word commands of most traditional adventure games.

The plot resembles most adventure games. There are trolls, magical items, and treasure galore. But this adventure game is a real pleasure to talk to. It almost seems human!

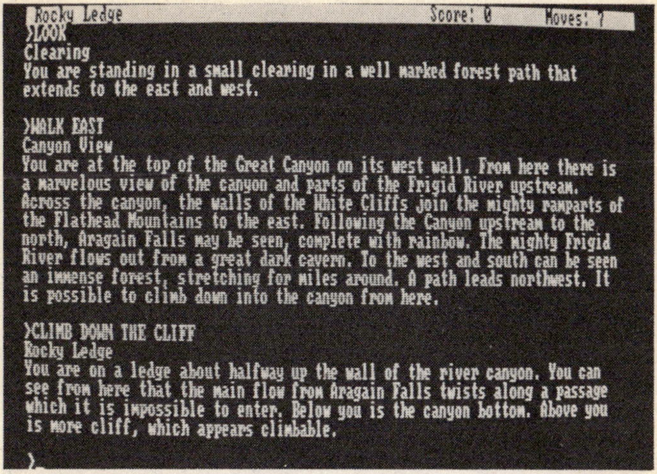

Rocky Ledge Score: 0 Moves: 7

>LOOK
Clearing
You are standing in a small clearing in a well marked forest path that extends to the east and west.

>WALK EAST
Canyon View
You are at the top of the Great Canyon on its west wall. From here there is a marvelous view of the canyon and parts of the Frigid River upstream. Across the canyon, the walls of the White Cliffs join the mighty ramparts of the Flathead Mountains to the east. Following the Canyon upstream to the north, Aragain Falls may be seen, complete with rainbow. The mighty Frigid River flows out from a great dark cavern. To the west and south can be seen an immense forest, stretching for miles around. A path leads northwest. It is possible to climb down into the canyon from here.

>CLIMB DOWN THE CLIFF
Rocky Ledge
You are on a ledge about halfway up the wall of the river canyon. You can see from here that the main flow from Aragain Falls twists along a passage which it is impossible to enter. Below you is the canyon bottom. Above you is more cliff, which appears climbable.

>

Figure 2.4 Zork I

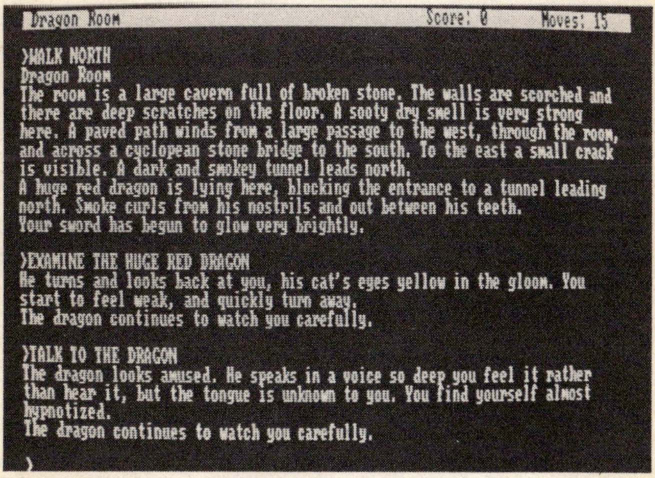

Dragon Room Score: 0 Moves: 15

>WALK NORTH
Dragon Room
The room is a large cavern full of broken stone. The walls are scorched and there are deep scratches on the floor. A sooty dry smell is very strong here. A paved path winds from a large passage to the west, through the room, and across a cyclopean stone bridge to the south. To the east a small crack is visible. A dark and smokey tunnel leads north.
A huge red dragon is lying here, blocking the entrance to a tunnel leading north. Smoke curls from his nostrils and out between his teeth.
Your sword has begun to glow very brightly.

>EXAMINE THE HUGE RED DRAGON
He turns and looks back at you, his cat's eyes yellow in the gloom. You start to feel weak, and quickly turn away.
The dragon continues to watch you carefully.

>TALK TO THE DRAGON
The dragon looks amused. He speaks in a voice so deep you feel it rather than hear it, but the tongue is unknown to you. You find yourself almost hypnotized.
The dragon continues to watch you carefully.

>

Figure 2.5 Zork II

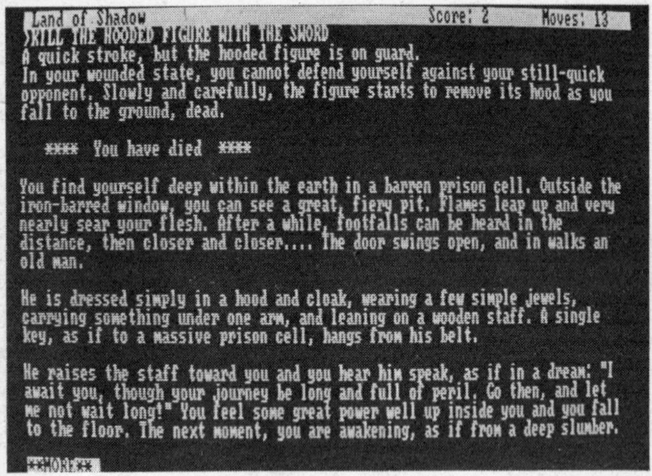

Figure 2.6 Zork III

Simulation Games

Simulation games are designed to mirror real-life experiences, like flying an airplane or running a large corporation. Some computerized simulations actually do prepare people for a real experience, such as flight simulators used by the Air Force or NASA, while others are purely for fun.

Deadline

Deadline is a unique game from Infocom ($49.95). Actually, we could have discussed this game in the fantasy-adventure category, but we really couldn't decide where to put it. It *is* an adventure, but in a sense it's also a simulation. It's a simulation of a detective's work, and it's really fun! This text-only game is head and shoulders above the early text-only games. What makes *Deadline* so much fun is the way it can understand so many different things you type in. This has become something of a trademark for Infocom.

Traditionally, text-only computer games for microcomputers have only been able to understand one or two-word commands. It can be terribly frustrating to continue to ask the same question in as many different two-word combinations as you can think of, only to have the program continue to tell you it doesn't understand your question. In this game, you are not restricted to two-word commands. You can type in things like "Put the knife in the trophy case," or "Unlock the door with the key," and the program understands perfectly. Of course, you can't talk to this program as you would to a friend, but its ability to understand a variety of commands and sentence structures is truly amazing!

Deadline puts you in the role of a tough detective out to solve the mystery of the death of Mr. Marshall Robner, millionaire industrialist and philanthropist. Robner was found dead on the floor of his library, the victim of an apparent overdose of the tranquilizer he had been taking. The door was locked

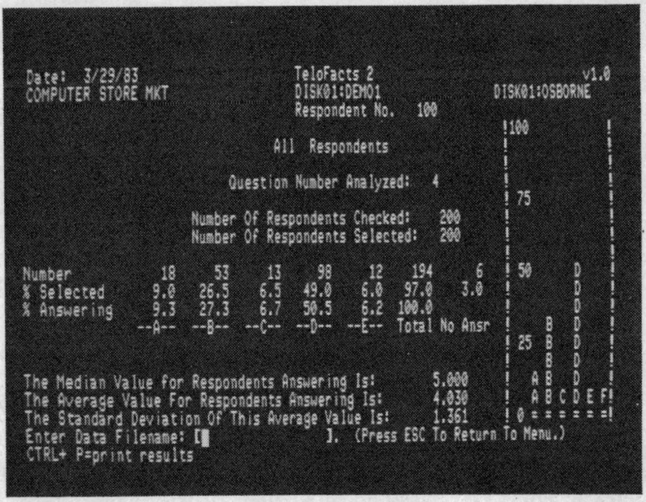

Figure 2.7 Deadline

from the inside. Robner had experienced recent business setbacks and had been suffering from severe bouts of depression. It seems to be an open-and-shut case of suicide. But is it? It's up to you to find out.

Robner's attorney is convinced there was no foul play, but he feels an investigation is in order, since Robner was in the process of changing his will when he died. Mrs. Robner is reluctant to cooperate, but grudgingly agrees to let you spend one day in the Robner mansion. Therefore, you have a deadline of twelve hours to complete your investigation and solve the case.

Each turn you take consumes one minute. A line at the top of the screen tells you how much time you have left. You are free to move around the Robner mansion and examine anything or anybody you please.

At first, the people you meet seem ordinary enough, but are they? There's Mrs. Robner, who was frequently visited by gentlemen callers and who is obviously NOT grief stricken over her husband's death. Then there is Ms. Dunbar, Robner's personal secretary, who seems to have been unusually close to Robner. And then there is George, the spoiled son who often quarreled with his father. You wonder too about Mr. Baxter, Robner's business partner, who may have more to gain from Robner's death than anyone suspects. There is also Mrs. Rourke, the housekeeper, who seems innocent enough, but who takes an unnatural interest in the personal affairs of everyone in the Robner household. There are other characters as well, and you are free to wander the estate, examine, question, fingerprint, and analyze to your heart's content. Meanwhile, the clock ticks on.

This is an elegant game, beautifully and artfully packaged. It comes complete with a letter of employment from Robner's attorney, a coroner's report, a photo of the death scene, a crime lab analysis of the teacup, a police report, a transcript of interviews with all the people concerned with the case, and even three of the "deadly pills" found near the body. In addition, there is a fine manual explaining how to play the game and how to talk to the program in language it will understand.

Figure 2.8 Contents of the Deadline Package

It will take most people about twenty hours to complete this game, and it can be saved at any point so that it can be resumed at a later time. Anyone who enjoys mysteries will love this Infocom game. It sets a new standard for text-only games. This one's a winner.

Suspended

This is another excellent simulation from Infocom (diskette—$49.95). Like *Deadline*, it has excellent packaging. The

Figure 2.9 Contents of the Suspended Package

game comes with a heavy playing board to help you keep track of what's going on.

The plot is a science fiction simulation. You were chosen by lottery to be placed in suspended animation, and your mind was used to control the life systems of an entire planet. This should have continued for 500 years. As the game begins, you have been unexpectedly awakened to cope with an emergency.

You must first determine what the emergency was, then deal with it.

You control six robots—Iris, Auda, Whiz, Waldo, Sensa, and Poet. Each of these robots has distinct strengths and weaknesses. Iris, for example, is highly visual but has limited mobility. Auda has unbelievably good hearing but is not equipped to carry out fine manipulations. You may address all of the robots at once or any one of them. Each will reply, and each seems to take on a personality of his or her own as the game develops.

This is another first-rate game. Like *Deadline*, the program understands a sizable vocabulary of complex sentences. Both games have been called *participatory novels*. That seemed a little outlandish before we really played these games. It doesn't anymore.

Spitfire Simulator

No section on simulations would be complete without at least one flying simulation. This one is available from Mind

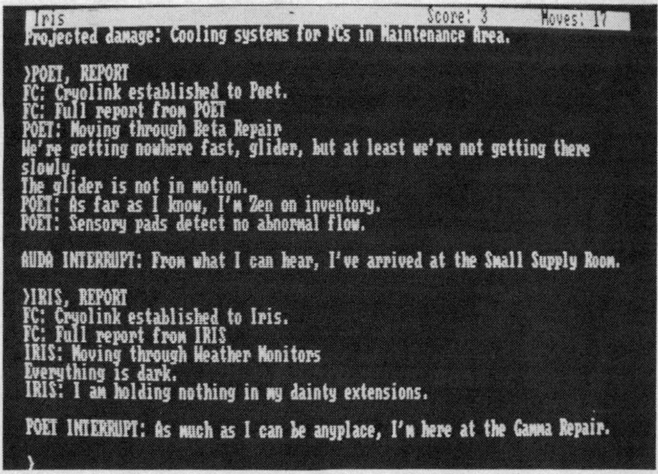

Figure 2.10 Suspended

Systems Corporation. You will need either game paddles or a joystick to play this $40.00 game.

The primary purpose of this simulation is entertainment, but flight education is a secondary purpose. The game features an out-the-window graphic view with flight instruments displayed below the window. Landings are so realistic you'll need practice to avoid catastrophe. After you master that, you can elect landings on super-short fields or engage in air-to-air combat.

This is a sophisticated flight simulation. It is definitely an adult program; you can learn a lot about flying by using it.

Napoleon's Campaigns

Napoleon's *Campaigns* is a classic war simulation available for $59.95 from Strategic Simulations, Inc.

The game can be played by one or two players who may choose the Waterloo or Leipzig campaign. Lines of commu-

Figure 2.11 Spitfire Simulator

nication are crucial and must be kept open if your orders are to be received. Even if the orders are received, there is a good chance they will be ignored. Once the battle begins, players may elect to act on initiative, withdraw on contact, stand, attack, or attack hastily. Points are earned by eliminating enemy headquarters or units. This is another complex simulation requiring logical thinking as well as accurate record keeping.

Strategic Simulations has many combat simulations, including *Computer Ambush*, a simulation that puts you in the role of a sergeant in the U.S. or German army during World War II. Your task is to command a squad of ten men who will fight hand-to-hand with the enemy squad. You can play against the computer or against a human opponent who controls the other squad.

Card Games, Las Vegas-Style Games, and Board Games

Casino

Casino is actually five different programs available on diskette for $39.95 from Datamost. The diskette contains blackjack, keno, poker, roulette, and baccarat. One of the nice touches is that you begin with $1000, and your balance is always current when you load the disk.

You can play many different opponents at all five games simultaneously, and you can order up instructions for any of the games at any time. The disk features music and the games are well-done.

Black Jack Strategy

Casino is designed for people who just want to play a little cards with a computer. *Black Jack Strategy* is designed for people who want to use their computer to learn something about playing cards.

Black Jack Strategy ($69.95) is available from Soft Images. You can play against this program, but the program will also

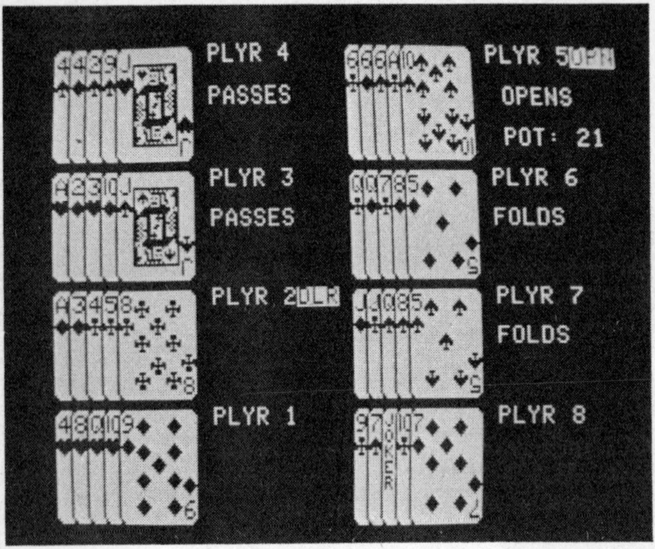

Figure 2.12 Pro Poker

set up certain card situations, monitor your play, and make suggestions aimed at improving it. All the basics are included, except card counting. A good manual is provided.

Pro Poker

Pro Poker is another of the *teaching* type of card program. The game is standard five-card draw, jacks or better, with up to eight real or computer-simulated players. One option causes the computer to offer strategic advice to you, another lets you see all the computer hands played face up. This game is available for $39.95 from Quality Software.

Other Card Games and Las Vegas-Type Games

Computer Gin Rummy, available for $29.95 from Datamost, includes three types of gin games.

Apple 21 is a blackjack game available for $24.95 from Softape.

King Cribbage is available for $24.95 from Hayden Book Company.

Board Games

Another staple of computer games is the type that simulates board games. The chess programs are well-developed, although no one has yet managed to come up with a chess program equal to a true chess master.

Chess 7.0

Larry Atkin's *Chess 7.0* is one of the better chess programs. This package is available from Odesta for $69.95. The graphics are excellent, and making your moves is quite simple. You first place the cursor on the piece you want to move, then press your game button or the return key. Next, you use the arrow keys to put the cursor where you want to move the piece, press the game button or the return key again, and the move is completed.

There are seventeen levels of play, but this program is far more than just an opponent. The computer can help you figure out the best moves and will show you thirty classic human and computer chess games. In addition, when you enter the program, you can choose to watch an excellent ten-minute tutorial on how to get the most out of the program.

Checkers and *Odin* are two other excellent programs available from the same company.

MicroGammon I

Microgammon II is available on disk for $19.95 from Softape. The graphics are excellent, doubling is possible, and the program is easy to use.

Monty Plays Scrabble and **Monty Plays Monopoly**

These game programs are available from Ritam Corp. and sell for $34.95 each. You need a traditional game set to play these games. You'll find the program a tough opponent, if you choose the more difficult levels of play.

Sports Games

There are many sports games available for your Apple computer. Many of these games are suitable for both children and adults, but you have to know the rules of each game.

Hi-Res Computer Golf

This highly acclaimed program is available for $29.95 from Avant-Garde Creations. Up to four players can play. You have five eighteen-hole courses to play on. The timing of your swing is the key in this game. The course presents sand traps and all the other trappings (no pun intended) in this fun game.

Hi-Res Computer Golf 2 sells for $34.95. It is the same game, modeled on three existing courses. You can select variable winds and an auto-swing mode if you want.

Other Sports Programs

Avalon Hill Microcomputer Games sells some very good sports programs. *Computer Football Strategy* and *Computer Statis Pro Baseball* are for one or two players and sell for $30.00 each. These are excellent games for adults or children. Ask for the Avalon Hill catalog if you are interested in other sports games. They have a very large selection, including many developed with *Sports Illustrated Magazine*.

WHERE TO LOOK FOR SOFTWARE

Apple software is carried by many computer stores and by an increasing number of computer software stores. Many bookstores also carry Apple software, particularly the large chains like B. Dalton and Waldenbooks. And new Apple programs of all types are reviewed in many of the popular computer magazines. *Creative Computing, Personal Computing*, *Compute!*, *inCider*, *Apple Orchard*, *Call APPLE*, and *NIBBLE* all publish good reviews of Apple software. In addition, many magazines like *Video Games* publish reviews of recreational software for the Apple. Two other good sources of reviews are *The Addison Wesley Book of Apple Computer Software for 1983*, and *The Blue Book for the Apple Computer* published by Scribner. Each book is more than 500 pages long and lists thousands of programs for your Apple, many of them games.

CHAPTER THREE

Arts and Crafts

You may not think of your computer as a musical instrument or an artist's canvas. After all, computers are machines, and machines aren't artistic, or are they? If you think your computer is only a number-crunching machine incapable of anything artistic, you may be in for a surprise. Sculptors have hammers and chisels, painters have pallettes and brushes, and musicians have pianos, electric guitars, or whatever. These are all tools artists use to create or play. The Apple IIe can also serve as a very useful tool for budding (or not so budding) artists and musicians. In this chapter we discuss several ways the computer can help you in your artistic endeavors.

The title of the chapter is not meant to imply that the applications discussed here will not be of interest to the professional person or to businesses. The Apple IIe is regularly used by businesses, for example, to design and generate all sorts of charts, figures, and tables. These *graphics* are used as overheads for meetings, in financial reports, and in accounting records. The major ways of using the computer for arts and crafts that we discuss here are:

- As an actual compositional medium. The computer and its peripherals serve as the musical instrument or the drawing pad.
- As a teaching machine. The computer assists in teaching

basic music and visual arts skills and in improving your understanding of music and art.

• As an expressive medium. The computer displays or plays what you have created.

The Apple IIe computer will not take the place of a baby grand piano or an electric organ. You will not be able to press a button and get a Picasso to hang on your wall. It probably won't take the place of music or art lessons either, but there are some very interesting things you can do with it in the areas of music and art. You can even create business graphics for reports and meetings more quickly, less expensively, and more professionally on a computer than in the traditional way.

Your Apple IIe is potentially a powerful graphics and sound machine. We say potential, because the computer normally displays no more than ordinary characters on its screen, and you usually hear no more than a high-pitched beep.

APPLE GRAPHICS

The Apple IIe divides its screen into 960 little squares. There are 40 squares on each of 24 different lines. Through the ordinary video display features of this computer, you can display upper and lowercase letters, numbers, punctuation marks, and several special symbols in any of those 960 squares. The Apple normally displays light characters on a dark background, but it can also display in *reverse video* (dark characters on a light background). And it's easy to make characters flash on and off.

A screen divided into only a few thousand squares is called a *low-resolution* screen. A particular square on the Apple IIe's screen may have a capital A, a lowercase h, a comma, or some other symbol in it. What the computer is actually displaying on the screen is a set of dots. Each character square on the screen is made up of a table of dot locations, eight dots wide and eight dots deep. If you look carefully at the information on the screen, you can probably see that each letter and character is not really a solid image but a pattern of closely-spaced dots. The Apple IIe creates all its low-resolution graphics and character displays by sending patterns of dots to the screen. Each of the 960 possible locations on the screen can display anything from a square where all of the 64 dots (eight rows of eight dots) are *off* (a blank square) to a square where all 64 dots are *on* (a solid square). By turning some of the dots on and some off, the Apple IIe can create patterns for all sorts of letters, numbers, symbols, and graphic characters. It is sort of like painting by numbers: you paint a picture by filling in the right areas with the right colors.

The disadvantage of low-resolution graphics is that you must work with large blocks of color. In its text mode, the Apple displays graphics or text in a 24-by-40 format. You can draw only relatively crude pictures and figures when each element is the size of a character; they'll have jagged edges and not a lot of detail. One of the Apple's low-resolution modes lets you divide the screen into 48 rows of 40 squares. That divides the screen into 1920 little rectangles. Those rectangles can be any of sixteen different colors. You get a better picture with the 48-by-40 format, but it's nothing to brag about.

A nice feature of the Apple computer is its provision for a few lines of text at the bottom of the screen when displaying graphics. That means you can put a maze or game board on the screen and still have room at the bottom of the screen for messages or directions. In addition, Apple's version of BASIC has several keywords in it such as PLOT, HLIN, and VLIN that make it easier to create your own graphics. HLIN stands for Horizontal Line, and VLIN is Vertical Line.

Virtually all of the great video-game graphics you see in Apple software use high-resolution (HI-RES) instead of low-resolution graphics. HI-RES graphics divide the screen into 280 rows with 192 dots on each row. That gives you 53760 picture elements (pixels) to use in creating graphics. With that many you can create some very detailed color graphics, with sharper images, smoother lines, and finer detail. Eight colors are available for use in HI-RES graphics.

Creating nice graphics on the Apple's screen is not as easy

with the unadorned Apple as it may sound. You either have to know a lot about computer programming, or you have to buy software designed to do much of the hard stuff for you.

Programs and Peripherals for Graphics

The popularity of the Apple and its built-in color graphics features has led many companies to develop software and hardware for Apple owners who want to use the computer for color graphics but don't want to spend hours writing programs.

Several simple graphics software packages let you move the cursor around on the screen by pressing the arrow keys on the keyboard. When you press the left arrow, the cursor moves left, when you press the right arrow, the cursor moves right, and so on. You can press one key to tell the computer that you want it to leave a trail of light as the cursor moves. In this way you can draw pictures or make designs on the computer screen by just moving the cursor. It is a lot like the Etch-A-Sketch toy that has been popular for years. A few of the better graphics software programs are reviewed below:

The Complete Graphics System

This graphics package is one of the best general-purpose systems available. It is easy to use and has a great deal of versatility. You can use either the keyboard or game paddles as your paint brush. You have over 100 colors to choose from and you can tell the computer to color in automatically any area you have drawn on the screen. A thorough manual goes into great detail on how to use the system and how to get started drawing your own pictures. The Complete Graphics system is sold by Penguin Software for $59.95.

Arcade Machine

This package falls into the very-easy-to-use category. It is entirely menu-driven and requires no programming ability. Using *Arcade Machine*, you can create shapes, give them colors, and move them around on the screen quickly and easily. It was actually designed to help people with few programming skills design professional-looking graphics for arcade-type games. The result was a software package that gives you an excellent way to explore the graphics capabilities of the Apple II without much computer experience.

The *Arcade Machine* is sold by Broderbund Software for $49, which is a very good price, considering the quality and flexibility of the software.

Graphics Magician

Graphics Magician actually does much more than just draw pictures on the computer screen. When you learn to use all of its many different modes and special features, you can make three-dimensional pictures and even create animations. This is not a beginner's program, however. You need to know some BASIC programming language to use it. Although not as simple to use as others, it is one of the most versatile graphics packages around. It is available from Penguin Software for $50.00.

Special Input and Output Devices for Graphics

Much of what you will want to do with graphics you can do with a good graphics software package and a dot matrix printer that can print graphics. A dot matrix printer creates characters on paper in a pattern of dots. Several popular printers, including the Epson MX-80 and FX-80 models, are often used with the Apple IIe to create printed copies of graphics displayed on the video screen. Several graphics software packages have special programs that let you create neat, non-standard character sets on your printer. For example, you can print Christmas letters to friends in Old English script or futuristic computer-style type. There are even a few printers, such as the IDS Prism 80, that print in color. With the appropriate software, you can draw a multicolored picture, chart, or figure on the screen of the computer and then get a printed copy of the screen graphics from your printer.

Color printers are relatively rare today and cost about twice as much as ordinary dot matrix printers. With a printer like the Epson MX-80 that costs less than $600, you can still get very good printed charts, figures, and black and white HI-RES graphics. If you want to print graphics as well as display them on the screen, be sure you check for printer and software compatibility. Some graphics programs for the Apple will work with only one or two models of dot matrix printers. Others won't work with any.

One of the least expensive and most versatile of graphics programs is called *Zoom Graphix*. This package is available for $39.95 from Phoenix Software Inc. *Zoom Graphix* makes printing your graphics easy and straightforward. It is menu-driven and has good easy-to-understand directions. One of the best features of the package is that it will work on a wide selection of printers.

There are also a variety of special peripheral devices designed just for doing graphics. *Plotters* and *printer/plotters* cost at least $800, usually more, and are used to create multicolored graphs and figures. Several business graphics software packages are available for the Apple IIe that work with plotters like the ones made by Houston Instruments, a division of Bausch and Lomb. With the appropriate software, you can use the Apple computer to create bar charts, graphs, and pie charts that look professionally drawn and labelled. Many plotters can draw on paper or on acetate overhead sheets in four to eight colors.

The HIPAD Digitizer. All of the art work we have told you about so far has to be done by using the keyboard and a programming language. Houston Instruments sells a device called *The HIPAD Digitizer*. This device, sometimes called a graphics tablet, has a flat eleven-by-seventeen-inch surface covered with a thick piece of embossed plastic. The digitizer comes with a pen-like stylus. When you move the stylus over the surface of the digitizer, the pattern is duplicated on the video screen. If you draw a circle, a circle is drawn on the screen. If you put a map of the United States on the digitizer and trace the border with the stylus, an outline of the U.S. will appear on the screen. The designs you create can be

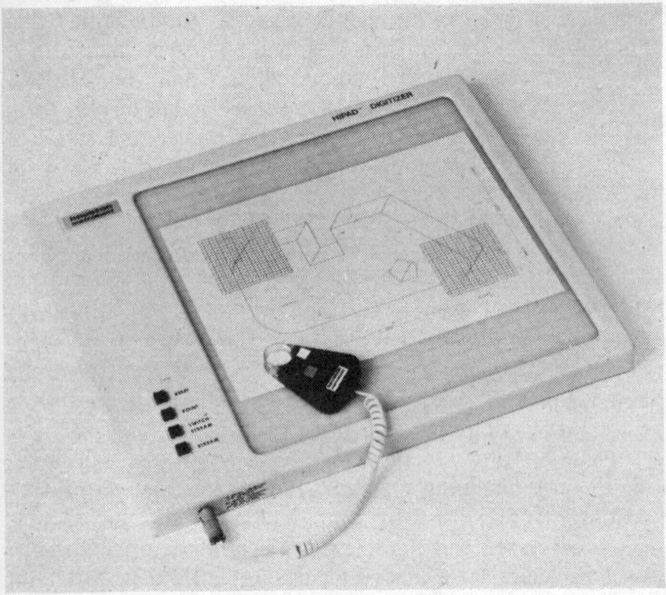

Figure 3.1 The HIPAD Digitizer

saved on a disk and used later in other programs. The digitizer gives you an easy, convenient way of creating good graphics. There are two problems with the HIPAD for simple graphics uses:

- It is very expensive ($825.00).
- It can be used only after some fairly complex programming has been done on the computer.

A much cheaper digitizer that comes with software that lets you start using it in a matter of minutes is *VersaWriter*, which sells for $299.00. After a brief installation and calibration procedure, you can use it much like the *HIPAD Digitizer*. The instrument manual is very good and explains the calibration procedure well. This system is sold by Versa Computing, Inc.

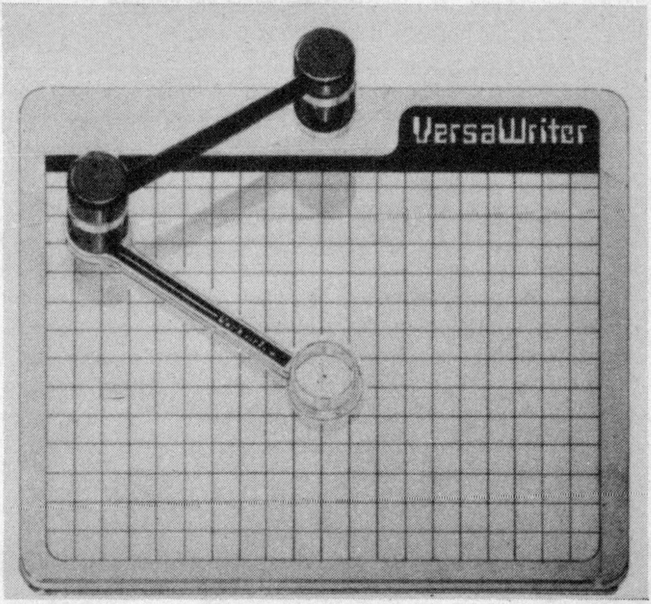

Figure 3.2 VersaWriter

SOUND

To understand just what can be done with computer-generated sound, you need to understand a few principles. In this section, we will explain some of the terms you'll come across when you read about computer-generated or synthesized sound and music.

Some Music Principles

• *Pitch* is determined by the frequency (cycles per second) of the sound. We hear cycles or waves created by vibrations in the air. These are measured in cycles per second, or Hertz. The typical human can hear sounds between 20 and 15,000 Hertz. Notes on a piano or any other musical instrument are organized by pitch. The sound created by a piano is organized into several *octaves*. A piano has slightly more than an eight-octave range from deep or bass sounds to high pitched notes. An octave is a group of sounds, rather than a single sound. It might begin with the C note and progress up through notes D, E, F, G, A, and B. The next C note ends that octave and begins the next highest octave. Composers and musicians have created a complicated system of naming sounds of different pitch and duration, but the primary difference between one note on a piano and another is the pitch (the Hertz of the sound.)

• *Amplitude* or *loudness* of the sound. We experience this as variations in the volume of the sound.

• *Duration* is the amount of time the sound is made. There are symbols and notation conventions that tell the musician exactly how much time to play each note in a composition.

• The *envelope* of the sound is the variation of loudness over the period it can be heard. Different sounds have different *attack* and *decay* patterns. Some reach their maximum loudness gradually and then trail off. Others begin at maximum amplitude and stop abruptly. The pattern of changes in amplitude of a tone help determine the timbre.

• *Timbre* is a musician's term for the complexity of the sound. Some sounds are pure tones, that is, they have only one pitch. Others have a major tone at a particular frequency and many harmonic or secondary frequencies that add richness to the sound. These secondary sounds are part of what gives each musical instrument its own personality.

Using the Apple II to Make Music

Much of the electronic music you hear on movie soundtracks and in concert performances is generated by very expensive computer-controlled sound synthesizers that can cost $15,000 or more. When we talk about computer-generated music, we are not limiting ourselves to these large systems. Small, inexpensive personal computers can also be made to generate music. Much of this capability depends on the software that is available, but some very serious musicians are using the Apple IIe and other personal computers as part of sophisticated systems for electronic music and sound effects.

Programming Your Own Music

The unadorned Apple IIe has a little device inside the case called a *sound generator*, which makes the beep when you turn on the computer. By controlling it, you can use the computer to generate sounds. The Apple is a relatively limited sound synthesizer, however. It is a *one-voice* system, which means only one sound can be generated at a time. Other computers let you generate as many as four separate sounds simultaneously. The Apple lets you control the pitch (over a limited range) and duration. The volume, timbre, and envelope of the sound cannot be controlled.

Software and Peripherals for Music

As with all types of software for the Apple IIe, a wide variety is available for music. Here's a sample of the music software you can get:

Music Maker

This program makes it easy to write songs that can be played through an Apple IIe's built-in speaker. *Music Maker* gives you a way to compose and play music on the computer without programming the computer yourself. The program lets you type in the notes for a song from the keyboard. You can play the piece you're composing at any time, even while you are entering the notes. Compositions can be edited and saved on disk for later use. As your song is playing, a display on the computer screen shows the current note number and gives you other information about the note. This method of having the computer step through the notes one by one makes it easy to spot errors, even in long songs or very fast passages.

The editor in this program works a lot like a word processor. You can insert notes into the song, or you can erase notes from the song, with simple keyboard commands. One nice feature is that, as you make changes, they are shown immediately. *Music Maker* comes with a well-written instruction manual containing a set of lessons for those inexperienced in the use of musical terms. Also included are complete instructions for using songs that are already stored on the program disk. *Music Maker* is sold by SubLogic for $29.95.

Electric Duet

This is another inexpensive music software package for the Apple IIe. As with *Music Maker*, you don't need a special music-synthesizer board, so you don't have to buy anything but the software. With this software alone, you can create, edit, and store on tape or on disk any song you write on the Apple IIe. *Electric Duet* puts out multivoice music with a variety of timbres. This means you are not limited to a single note at a time but can have the computer play two or more notes at the same time. The sound quality you get from the Apple IIe with this program is not as good as that produced with specially-designed hardware. However, it is acceptable for many purposes, especially when you consider the low cost.

There are three modes of operation:

- Jukebox mode. You use this mode to play various musical numbers stored on the disk when you buy it. These numbers include Classical pieces such as Mozart's *Sonata in C Major* and two of Bach's *Inventions*.

- Piano mode. Use this mode to enter and play music from the keyboard. The keys are assigned note values and arranged like the keys on a piano. The top two rows of keys correspond to the higher notes, and the bottom rows correspond to the lower notes.

- Music editor mode. You use this mode to edit the music as you put it on the computer screen.

The entire program is *menu-driven*, which means options are listed on the screen, and all you have to do is select the option you want. *Electric Duet* is sold by Insoft; the entire package costs only $29.95.

ALF Apple Music Synthesizer

This is an easy-to-use peripheral-and-software combination you can use to program music into an Apple IIe computer using standard musical notation. The ALF kit includes the synthesizer board, the software, and an instruction manual. This system will do everything that the other two systems will do, but with higher quality. Because the system uses its own musical sound generator, instead of relying on the sound system built into the Apple IIe, the sound is richer and fuller. The difference is as great as that between a toy trumpet and a professional trumpet. The ALF system, which has been around for some time, is a sophisticated sound system for both composing and playing electronic music. The *ALF Music Synthesizer* is sold by Peripherals Plus for $198.00.

Keyboard Music with the Apple II

One obvious difference between creating music on a computer and on an instrument like a piano or organ is the lack of a piano-style keyboard on the computer. When you sit down to any standard keyboard instrument, you don't have to worry about how to make a single note sound long or short. You just hold down a key for as long as you want it to sound. The computer, on the other hand, has to be told everything about each note it generates: how high, how loud and how long. Telling the computer all that often requires the use of a complicated coding system. Consequently, you cannot use the keyboard of your computer the same way you use the keyboard of your electric organ. You can get around this problem by

Figure 3.3 You can't really play this one, but with music cards from ALF Products, Inc., you can explore the world of music.

buying a keyboard device for your computer. These devices are quite expensive and can be justified only if you really want to use the Apple IIe for serious music.

The SOUNDCHASER Computer Music System. One of the least expensive keyboard systems available for the Apple IIe is *The SOUNDCHASER Computer Music System* manufactured by Passport Designs, Inc. There are a lot of options with this system, so you will want to do some investigating to make sure you are getting just what you need. Basically, it includes a piano-style keyboard and software that converts the electronic signals sent by the keyboard into signals the computer can recognize. Depending on which features you want, one of these systems will cost from $1000 to $1350.

Figure 3.4 ENTRY program screen display from ALF Products, Inc.

Figure 3.5 AlphaSyntauri System

The AlphaSyntauri System. If you are really serious about music with the Apple IIe, you can join famous musicians like Herbie Hancock, who uses an *AlphaSyntauri* keyboard system in performing much of his famous jazz music. This system has many options, like the *SOUNDCHASER*, but will cost you more, between $1295 and $1995. For further information on this system write Syntauri Corporation.

Both the *AlphaSyntauri* and *SOUNDCHASER* systems let you create electronic music from the piano-style keyboard. The music you compose can be played by the sound synthesizer as you press the keys, it can be stored on a disk and played or edited later. These are sophisticated, professional-quality peripherals for the Apple IIe that enhance its musical talents considerably.

Music Training

Some software packages use the music capabilities of the computer to put it in the role of a music teacher. Programs that use the computer as a music-teaching tool are generally drill and practice programs. They do things like sound a note and have the student name the note. Or they play a short melody and then have the student program the same melody back into the computer. Several such programs are reviewed below:

Ear Training. Peripherals Plus, the company that sells the *ALF Music System*, also has a series of ear training software, called *Ear Training*. You can use these programs to learn many musical skills. This system sells for $449.95.

Apple Music Theory. One of the most comprehensive software packages for music training is *Apple Music Theory* from the manufacturer of the computer. This is a series of clever programs that make it fun to learn music fundamentals. They were developed for Apple by a group of Minnesota music teachers. The programs use lots of good graphics along with the instruction, so you hear and see the music as it is being played. To use the system, you will need an Apple IIe, an Apple IIe disk drive system, and a good color monitor. The suggested price is $50.

Pick That Tune. This simple program was designed primarily as a party game. It can accommodate as many as ten players at one time. The computer begins playing the notes of a tune, and the players try to guess the title. There's an elaborate scoring system and a good selection of tunes. *Pick That Tune* is available from Swearingen Software for $29.95.

CHAPTER FOUR

The Apple II as Teacher

Much is made of the ability of small computers such as the Apple to function as educational devices in the home and classroom. The computer is only the latest in a long list of technological inventions that were supposed to revolutionize education in the twentieth century. In spite of the attention computers receive in the educational press, we do not believe they are likely to revolutionize the little red schoolhouse overnight. However, there is good reason to expect that education will evolve quickly in the coming years. There are two reasons for this: the decentralization of education and the need for lifelong learning.

THE DESCHOOLING OF LEARNING

Education has been institutionalized for most of the twentieth century. Learning has been something children do in a classroom supervised by one or more adults. This model will continue to be important through the end of this century, but by the year 2000 it will play a smaller role than it does today. More people will spend time learning at home, in the office, at the factory, and at adult learning centers. Learning will be a lifelong task rather than something children do to prepare for adulthood.

In earlier times you could learn a trade or profession and then earn your livelihood for the rest of your life with the skills you acquired. Today virtually every job is being changed or eliminated by new information, new social trends, or new technology. Physicians, for example, cannot continue practicing medicine for years without keeping up with new discoveries that affect the way they practice. Like the wagon-wheel factory that converts to hubcaps, many of us will have to learn a different profession or trade at least once in our lifetime. Most of us will find ourselves learning throughout our lives to keep up with change. Many of us will return to some sort of adult training program to retool for a new profession.

Even if your job stays stable, there are many other aspects of your life that will change. Consider our federal income tax. Changes in the federal income tax laws can mean thousands of dollars to families with modest incomes. Failure to keep up with these changes can be an expensive oversight.

Figure 4.1 Learning together in the classroom

Figure 4.2 Learning with computers happens in the home, too.

We must continue to learn, regardless of our age, if we are to cope with the demands of life. And in the future all of us will spend more time in learning activities in our homes and workplaces. Fortunately, small computers like the Apple can be helpful in both traditional and non-traditional learning environments. For example, families will be able to buy computer programs that teach them about new income tax laws. Several programs for the Apple even computerize record keeping for income tax and the actual completion of the forms.

THE SMALL COMPUTER AS A TEACHING MACHINE

There are many ways computers can help you and your children learn. Currently most students, from elementary school to college, have little or no contact with computers during their educational careers. This will change drastically in the coming years, because computers are becoming integral parts of thousands of jobs. Few people will be able to find jobs that are not influenced, in one way or another, by computers.

Computer Literacy

This brings us to the first use of a computer: as a means of becoming computer literate. Although children tend to take to computers naturally, many adults are not at ease with them. They feel uncomfortable around them and do not look forward to the time when computers are an appliance in the home and office.

Buying and using a computer like the Apple is one very effective way of overcoming that initial feeling of discomfort. It is a good way to learn how the computer operates, what it can and can't do. Becoming computer literatc is perhaps the most important cducational benefit of owning a computer.

You may think computer literacy is silly because it implies understanding computers is like learning to read. Reading is an essential skill in this society, while computer literacy is not. The universal need to be able to read is a relatively modern concept, however. Two hundred years ago well over ninety-nine percent of the worlds's population could not read. Yet these illiterate people were able to deal with their day-to-day demands. Arguing that everyone should be taught to read probably sounded silly in the 1700's. Today we believe the next generation should be taught to read because our society requires it. You cannot cope with life today as a responsible adult without that skill.

The shift from an *industrial* society to an *information* society will continue. That development will bring us rapidly to the point where computer literacy is just as essential to modern living as the ability to read.

Computer-Assisted Instruction

Computer-Assisted Instruction (CAI), Computer-Aided Learning (CAL), and Computer-Aided Instruction (CAI) are all terms that refer to the use of computers in education. We will use the abbreviation CAI to refer to several types of computer-based teaching approaches that give some of the responsibility for teaching to the computer. There are three general types of CAI: drill and practice, tutorial, and simulations.

Drill and Practice

The simplest type of computer-assisted instruction is drill and practice. Drill and practice programs don't really teach you anything; they just help you practice something you've already learned. A common type of drill and practice helps you practice basic math skills. The computer generates a problem and asks the student to type in the answer. When you respond, the computer lets you know whether the answer was correct or incorrect.

A more sophisticated type of drill and practice program keeps track of your errors, explains them, and provides help. New problems are adjusted to your current needs. Some drill and practice programs set the difficulty level of problems on the basis of your performance during earlier sessions. Several Apple drill and practice are described later in this chapter.

Tutorial Programs

A tutorial program does more than just give you practice on something you already know. It actually teaches. Educational programs that use the tutorial format are more difficult to write than those that use the drill and practice format. You must teach the skill, evaluate learning, and provide practice. There are a few good tutorial programs for the Apple.

Simulations

When you drop a quarter into an arcade game and control an interstellar fighter with laser guns and force-field shields, you are participating in a computer simulation.

Simulations are models of often complex events or conditions. You take a role in the simulations and help determine what happens next by the decisions you make. A computer simulation is an imaginary environment with its own rules. In an educational simulation, you take a role in the imaginary environment, for example, as the king of an ancient kingdom, the president of a large manufacturing company, or the operator of a small retail business. In a popular simulation called *Hammurabi*, you are the ruler of an ancient city that has 100 citizens, 1000 acres of land for cultivation, and 3000 bushels of grain in storage. You must decide how much grain to give the people to eat, how much to save for seed, and how many acres to plant. Your decisions determine whether the kingdom starves, or grows and develops (and requires more grain next year).

Simulations are widely used in business and industry. Nuclear and chemical plant workers are trained by computer simulations. It is much less expensive to have a trainee blow up a make-believe plant on the computer screen than to make a real mistake.

They are useful in teaching basic skills, concepts, and attitudes. Some are not only effective training tools; they are also fun. Many of the popular computer and arcade games are simulations designed for fun rather than learning. As we noted in Chapter Two, many of the popular video games have some educational aspects.

Other Educational Applications

Computer literacy, drill and practice, tutorial programs, and simulations account for the majority of computer applications in education today. Another approach, Computer-Managed Instruction (CMI), uses the computer as a manager or overseer of learning. For example, students may be given a series of assignments that require them to read a text and work in the library. As each assignment is finished, the student sits at the computer and takes a test on the assignment. A "pass" means the student can go on to the next assignment. Otherwise, the computer provides suggestions for further study.

CMI requires quite a lot of work from the teacher to set up, but it does not require the teacher to actually write programs that teach the student. The teacher can use an *authoring language* to develop both CAI and CMI programs, rather than learning to program the computer in a language like BASIC. Several authoring languages are available for the Apple, and the PILOT language is also often used by teachers who want to develop their own CAI or CMI. Several authoring languages and at least three versions of PILOT are available for the Apple.

Logo, a popular language developed at the Massachusetts Institute of Technology, is also used in education. It is considered by many to be an ideal first language for children. Advocates say it does more than provide children with an enjoyable, even exciting, way to learn to program a computer. It also helps them develop better, more sophisticated ways of thinking and solving problems. Parents and teachers who would like to read a strong statement of support for Logo by its developer should read Seymour Papert's book, *Mindstorms*. A less enthusiastic, but still positive, view of the language is given in *Computers, Teaching, and Learning*, a book published by dilithium Press and written by Jerry Willis, LaMont Johnson, and Paul Dixon.

The computer can also be a versatile *tool* in the classroom or at home. We use many tools in our efforts to learn. There are, of course, pens, pencils, tablets, rulers, and protractors. Specialized classes such as chemistry, biology, or typing also have their own sets of tools—Bunsen burners, flasks, test tubes, scales, scalpels, and typewriters. The computer's role as an educational tool is likely to grow in the future. English students will use its word processing power to write term papers, students in physics and chemistry will use it to calculate complicated formulas, and math students are likely to find it integrated into math courses.

EDUCATIONAL SOFTWARE

Educational programs currently available for the Apple include drill and practice, tutorials, and simulations.

Drill and Practice and Tutorial Programs

Arcademics

This is a series of six disks that combine some of the characteristics of arcade action games with drill and practice. They were developed by the DLM company, major producers of special education materials. *Dragon Mix*, *Alligator Mix*, *Alien Addition*, *Demolition Division*, *Minus Mission*, and *Meteor Multiplication* each sell for $39.00, or you can buy the entire set for $220.00. Each package includes a teacher's manual, a disk, duplication masters, and a set of flashcards.

DLM aims these drill and practice packages at schools, but parents buy them, too, because they provide lots of motivation to practice basic skills. These programs are a creative blend of education and games.

In *Meteor Multiplication*, you are given a multiplication problem. Your task is to blast the asteroid containing the correct answer. When the game begins, you are immediately presented with a high-quality color graphic of your star station in the center of the display. The star station is surrounded by eight colorful asteroids rapidly converging on the station. In the center of each asteroid is a multiplication problem such as 6x6 or 4x2. In the background a clock is ticking. With each tick, one of the asteroids blinks and moves one step closer to the space station. Then you can use the arrow keys to rotate the space station until its laser gun is pointed at the approaching asteroid. You fire the laser by pressing the space bar. If you have typed in the correct answer, the asteroid disintegrates when you hit it, complete with satisfying sound effects. If the answer is wrong, the laser fires, but the asteroid continues to advance on the station. You must destroy all the asteroids before they reach the station. If any asteroid reaches the space station, you lose. Hits and misses are recorded at the bottom of the screen. High and low scores are displayed periodically.

This is an excellent drill and practice math game. The task is very challenging. We played the game for about ten minutes and only once managed to wipe out all the asteroids.

In *Demolition Division*, five tanks displaying division facts move toward five artillery emplacements on the right side of the screen. As the tanks advance, they fire their guns at a wall protecting each gun emplacement. You enter an answer beside one of your guns and hit the space bar. If the answer is too large, your shot lands behind the tank. If the number is too short, the shot falls in front of it. If the number is the correct answer to the problem displayed by the tank, the tank is destroyed. You must work quickly, because as soon as any wall

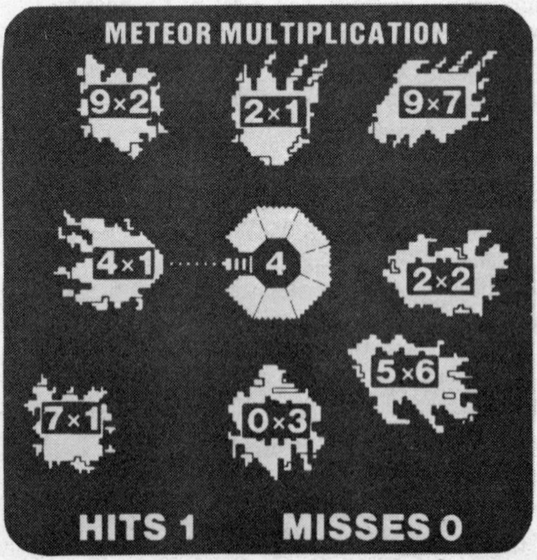

Figure 4.3 Meteor Multiplication

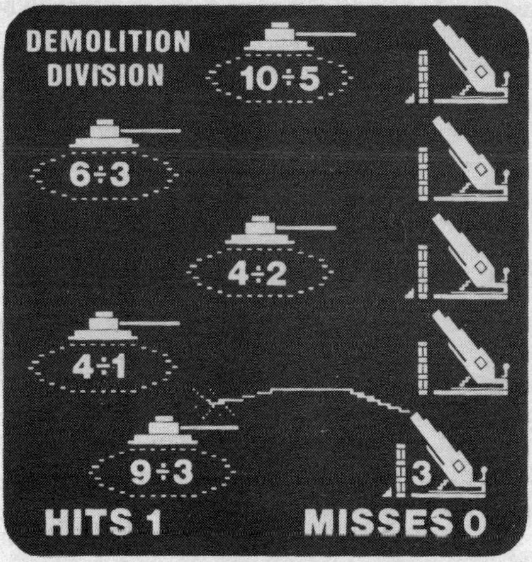

Figure 4.4 Demolition Division

is totally destroyed by a tank, the next shot will wipe out the gun emplacement, and you lose the game.

Dragon Mix provides practice in both multiplication and division facts. A large dragon on the right of the screen is defending a city with skyscrapers in the background. Three alien ships are approaching the dragon. Each ship has a different multiplication or division problem embedded in it. Answers appear in the center of the dragon. You must match the answer to the approaching ship, aim the dragon's tongue at it, and hit the space bar. If you choose the correct ship, it will be destroyed. If you make the wrong choice, the ship just keeps coming. If a ship gets close enough, it begins to wipe out the city. Three hits on the city and you lose.

The other programs are similar in format. Arcade-style action graphics and sound effects are used to keep children (or adults) motivated.

Each program lets you change the game if you want to. Speed of the action, difficulty of the problems, time for each game, and whether the keyboard or game paddles will be used can all be changed to suit your needs.

This is a unique series of programs. The graphics and sound effects are first-rate. Some sound educational thinking went into the programming. Finding educational software incorporating both excellent programming and educational content is rare. DLM has it.

College Board SAT Exam Preparation Series

This six-disk series ($299.95) contains over forty programs designed to help you improve your score on the Scholastic Aptitude Test (SAT), the test used by many American colleges to help them determine who will be admitted as students. These programs generate practice questions similar to those used on the SAT. The computer is also programmed to give you quick feedback on how you're doing.

The series is from Krell Software Corporation, and it's one

Figure 4.5 Dragon Mix

of the best drill and practice programs we have ever seen. Once one of the disks is loaded into the computer, it is simplicity itself to use the programs. Menus are presented when lessons are started or finished, and instructions are easy to understand.

Krell is so sure that their program will result in improved performance on the SAT, they issue a warranty. It promises to refund the full purchase price of the software if you use the programs but fail to increase your score by at least seventy points.

The six disks contain drill and practice on skill areas tested by the SAT, including math, vocabulary, written English, word relationships, reading comprehension, and sentence completion. Two of the disks contain the math programs, two contain the English programs, one contains the vocabulary programs, and one contains word relationships, reading comprehension, and sentence completion.

You may choose to use the *automatic learning strategy* for any of the programs. If you choose this option, the program analyzes your performance on an ongoing basis and uses that information to change the way problems are selected for you. This helps give you work at the level where you need help—not too hard and not too easy.

You can use another option, the *worksheet generator*, if you have a printer to produce a written copy of the problems rather than a screen display of them. The *worksheet generator* also prints an answer sheet.

At the end of each session, you can choose to be shown a screen display or a printout telling you how you did on each type of skill covered by that lesson.

This is an excellent way to practice for the SAT. If you are hoping to improve your score, this program should help.

Krell is planning another interesting package for release in 1984. Called *Complete Classroom Tutorial Package*, this series of programs will go beyond drill and practice to provide detailed instruction in the specific skill areas you need to do well on the SAT. If Krell does as good a job on this tutorial package as it has done on its drill and practice package, this one will be another winner!

Essential Mathematics I, II, III

Micro School Programs–Bertamax, Inc., produces a large number of excellent drill and practice math programs. There are nearly 600 lessons in this series of approximately 58 programs. Most parents will not be interested in purchasing the entire series. *Series I* and *II* sell for $56.80 each; *Series III* will soon be available, but no price has been set. The lessons at grade levels six through eight are divided into strands dealing with decimals and percents, fractions, number concepts, and pre-algebra. These are sold separately for $69.80 each or as an entire package for $275.00.

The lessons use some graphic displays, but they are not highly sophisticated. The emphasis is on the mathematical content rather than on arcade-like features. As an example of how graphics are used, lessons in grades one and two feature visual helps. When you press a key, objects are pictured on the screen. You may count these objects to get the answer to a problem.

These lessons are typical drill and practice programs and can be quite helpful. They are not inspiring or revolutionary, but this series has some continuity and can provide thorough practice on needed skills.

MasterType

The Universe is not always kind to those who type slowly. There is hope, however, for those who carefully read this manual. It is your guide to survival in interstellar combat.

So begins the *MasterType* manual. This is another program that uses arcade action to help teach you a skill. There are eighteen lessons aimed at teaching you to type. Each lesson teaches a different touch-typing skill. At the beginning of each lesson, the screen tells you what is being studied and gives you instructions on how good typists use that skill.

Most lessons put you in the middle of a screen as a large blue command ship. You are being attacked by smaller enemy ships, usually from all four corners of the screen. A word or letter appears in each corner of the display. You must type that word or letter when it appears briefly in the center of your ship. If you have typed it correctly, a bolt of energy flashes out from your ship and destroys one of the attackers. You can't relax, however, because the ships keep coming, and new things to type keep appearing. If an attacker gets close enough to touch your ship, *goodbye*, *ship*. The program keeps score, the graphics are excellent, and the sound effects are first-rate. This is an outstanding program.

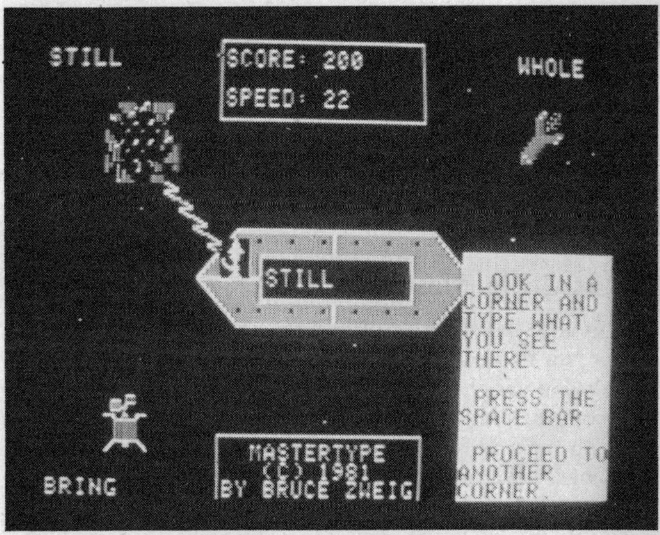

Figure 4.6 MasterType

Microbe

This innovative simulation makes good use of the Apple's color graphics features. The program ($44.95 on disk from Synergistic Software) is subtitled "The Anatomical Adventure." It puts students in the role of the commander of the Microbe, a microminiature submarine that has been injected into the bloodstream of a patient who is in serious trouble.

Your job is to make your way through the bloodstream of the patient, find the problem, correct it, and get out alive.

This program plays like a video game, but the information and skills you need to master the game include knowledge about human anatomy, particularly the circulatory system. Your ship may be attacked by microbes, it can get lost in an artery, and you can be attacked by all sorts of bacteria and parasites. You must identify the attackers, prescribe an appropriate remedy (for instance, release antibiotics), and take care to maintain the health of the patient.

The graphics are very good, and the program is one of the better of the *educational simulations* available today.

There are several levels of difficulty in the game, more than one person can play, and it even has speech output. If your Apple is equipped with one of the more popular speech synthesis boards, such as the Votrax Type N Talk or the Echo-GP. The program comes with several good manuals; we recommend it.

Knowledge Master

This disk-based series of programs from Academic Hallmarks is a real contrast to the other educational simulations described in this chapter. *Knowledge Master* programs are really disks of hundreds of multiple-choice and short-answer questions on many different topics. You use these programs by selecting a topic and the number of questions to be asked, then taking a test over the topic. There are questions on historical, scientific, academic, and current events topics. For example, there are questions on World War II.

The programs are well-written and well-executed. The graphics aren't great, and all you are really doing is answering lots of questions. Still, they are interesting and enjoyable. Whoever wrote the program and the manual had a good sense of humor. The programs can give you quizzes on a particular topic, or you can play against another person, with each person having a turn at answering a question. You can even add your own list of questions if you wish. We liked the program. Each disk costs $27.00; subject series vary from three disks for $63.00 to eight disks for $172.00.

Computer Advanced Ideas Educational Programs

Computer Advanced Ideas is a new company that has several educational programs designed for the home and school market. One of their programs, *Master Match* ($39.95), simulates a popular television game show. The top of the screen is a set of numbered boxes. The object of the game is to match the information in two boxes and thus score points. For example, one version of the game is on U.S. geography. Some boxes have the shapes of states and others have the names of states. You select two boxes each time you have a turn. If they match (shape of state with name), you earn a point. You see the contents of the boxes for only a few seconds, so you must

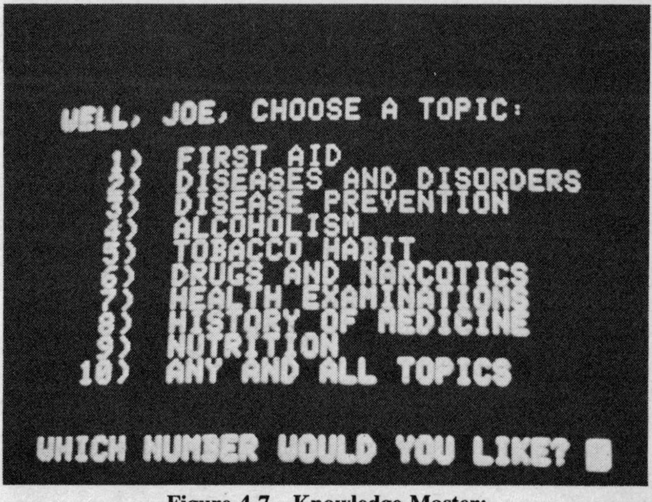

Figure 4.7 Knowledge Master: choices available under the health program

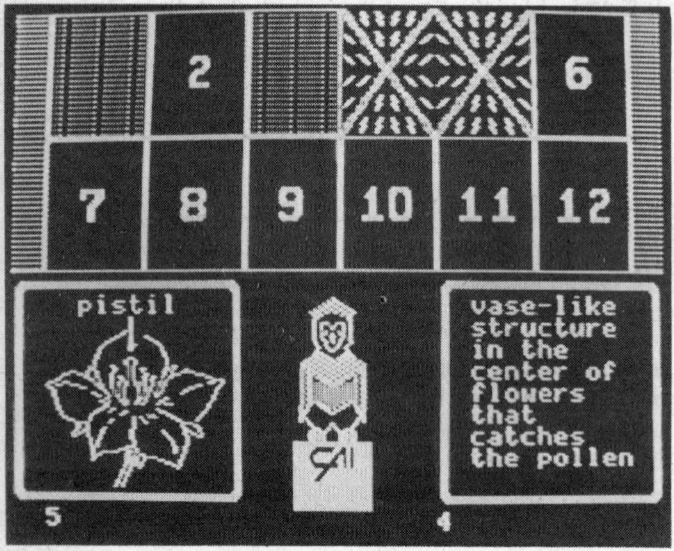

Figure 4.8 Master Match

remember what is in each of the boxes already selected. The game has good color, animated graphics, and an appealing game format. Topics you can select for the game include pattern recognition, animal sounds, directionality, count and match, opposites (Spanish), German travel words, and U.S. geography. *Master Match* is $40; additional disks that let you play the game using other topics are $20.

Another game from Computer Advanced Ideas is *The Game Show*. It uses the format of a popular television quiz show. *The Game Show* works like the board game Password. You play with an animated teammate on the screen, either Joe or May, and a quizmaster who gives them words. They give you a clue, and you guess what the word is. You can select topics such as vocabulary, animals, algebra, computer terms, sailing terms, Constitution, nursery rhymes, biology, and famous cities. Additional disks of subject words and clues are also available on lower and higher-level vocabulary words, people-places-

and-things, and movies-and-television. As the game is played, you get a turn, and your teammate gives you a clue. You make a guess. Points are awarded to your team if you get it right; the other team gets a turn (and another clue) if you get it wrong. Kids, and many adults, love this program because it is a game. Teachers and parents like it because it is has educational value. The game has very good color graphics and sound effects. It costs $40.00 and additional disks with more topics are $20.00 each. We recommend it.

Finally, Computer Advanced Ideas has a program called *Tic Tac Show*. This is another game with very good color graphics and animation. It is played like regular Tic Tac Toe, except you must answer a question before you get your X or O put on the grid. If you miss the question, your opponent gets that square. It is $40, and disks that add questions from other topic areas are $20.

Figure 4.9 The Game Show

Figure 4.10 Tic Tac Show

The Learning Company Program

The Learning Company has been involved in writing educational software for several years and has become one of the most innovative of the hundreds of companies writing programs today. Most of the programs from The Learning Company are interactive, interesting games with very good color graphics and sound. The innovation of The Learning Company's programs is not in their color graphics or sound effects, however. It is in the educational goals they accomplish. Most of the programs are aimed at concepts and strategies, not simply at facts and figures. Children who play these games often learn something other than the year of the Battle of Hastings or the shape of the state of Maine. Those facts may be important, and there is nothing wrong with writing programs that teach them. There are lots of *facts and figures* programs around today, though. There are only a few programs that teach concepts and problem-solving strategies.

One program from The Learning Company is *Rocky's Boots*. (disk—$19.95) It uses a video game concept to teach Boolean algebra and computer integrated circuit concepts. You learn about AND, OR, and NOT gates, and about FLIP FLOPS, CLOCKS, and DELAY circuits.

Your guide as you learn about all these things is Rocky Raccoon and his electric boots. He teaches you about the components that make up a computer. He doesn't deal with the actual components such as resistors, capacitors, and integrated circuits, however. He covers the conceptual components such as AND gates, FLIP FLOPS, and NOT gates. One part of the program lets you build circuits made up of the same conceptual components that make up a real computer. You see those circuits in color on the screen and you can actually use them by entering data and watching what happens as the data moves from one selection of the circuit to another. Once you've mastered the basics of logic gates and Boolean algebra, you can play several video games that require your new knowledge. There is also a game that lets you wander through a fifteen-room adventure using your joystick to travel from room to room. Again, your knowledge of computer logic is required to survive the adventure. Finally, *Rocky's Boots* lets you design your own game.

This is an excellent educational game. Some teachers (and perhaps parents) who try to load the program and run it have been very critical because it seems confusing and illogical. That's because they don't know the logic behind the program and haven't read the manual. *Read the manual*; then look at the program. It's great. We need more programs like this one.

Other programs from The Learning Company include *Bumble Games* and *Bumble Plot*, a set of games that teach young children number concepts and graphing; *Juggles' Rainbow*, which teaches the concepts of up, down, left, and right to young children; *Moptown*, a program that teaches sound thinking strategies; *Gertrude's Puzzles* and *Gertrude's Secrets*, which teach logic and problem-solving strategies.

Programs from The Learning Company are examples other companies should emulate.

Xerox and Stickybear

Xerox Educational Publications and Weekly Reader have collaborated to produce a series of educational programs that are a cut above the competition. Most of the programs feature a portly but happy bear called Stickybear who accompanies you through the program. Most of the Xerox programs are for young children, they have outstanding graphics, good sound effects, and interesting formats. *Stickybear Numbers* ($40.00) teaches young children, three to six, number concepts. The numbers from zero to nine are covered. When a child presses one of the number keys on the keyboard, the screen fills with great color graphics of things like rockets, arrows, waddling penguins, or trains with their smokestacks puffing smoke. If you press 3, you get three items; press 5 and five appear. Stickybear appears in many of the screen displays. He may be eating ice cream or watching bouncing balls, and so on. There are several variations of the program, but the basic idea is to teach children the quantity concept associated with the number symbols. It does that while entertaining children marvelously.

Stickybear ABC ($40.00) does the same job with letters of the alphabet. Press a letter key, and something on the screen shows up that begins with that letter. If you press the same letter again, something else associated with that letter appears. X, for example, shows Stickybear behind a machine getting an X-ray. Press I, and a table with ice cream on it appears, and Stickybear rises up slowly from under the table and looks longingly at the ice cream.

Stickybear Bop ($40.00) is a video game with several levels. It is animated, with color graphics and sound. You use the keys on the keyboard to shoot at moving targets in an arcade or to catch balls being juggled by Stickybear.

Finally, *Old Ironsides* ($40.00) is a simulation of a sea battle during the War of 1812. All these programs from Xerox are very good. Their animation is some of the best around, and the color displays are better designed and more appealing than

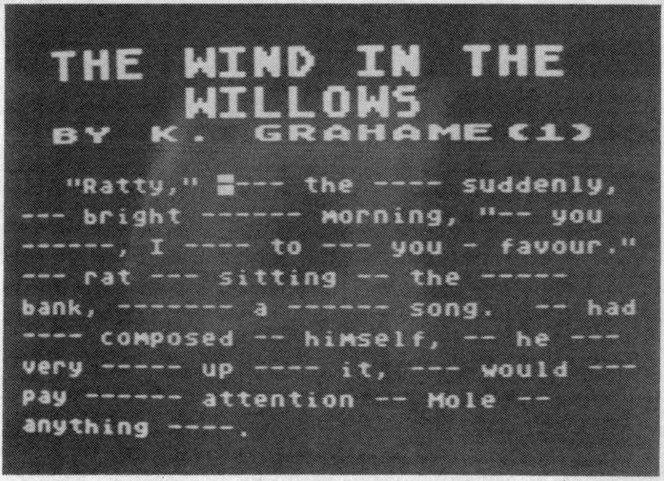

Figure 4.11 M-SS-NG L-NKS

ninety-nine percent of the displays in both educational software and video games. This is a very good series of programs.

M-SS-NG L-NKS and Other Programs

Sunburst Communications sells over fifty language arts programs for children and adults. *M-SS-NG L-NKS* is really a language puzzle that lets students discover and put to work implicit language skills they may not even know they have. It comes in seven versions: Young People's Literature, Literary MicroAnthology, MicroEncyclopedia, English Editor, German Editor, Spanish Editor, and French Editor.

In all versions, children fill in the blanks in words and sentences using knowledge about the succession of letters in words, words in sentences, and the meaning of the whole.

This series of language programs was designed by a group of people who are experts in how children acquire language. The theory behind these programs is sound, the lessons are interesting and well-done, and we recommend them highly.

Other Apple programs available from Sunburst are *Survival*

Math (disk—$50.00) and *Teasers by Tobbs* (disk—$35.00). *Survival Math* has some interesting simulations, such as putting your child in charge of a hot dog stand. We'll talk about that program later.

Teasers by Tobbs is a group of logic and math puzzles and problem-solving exercises. Sunburst has a large number of other educational programs available in the $25–$60 price range. Write for a catalog if you're interested.

How to Program in the BASIC Language

This set of programs is available on cassette or diskette ($74.95) from Sterling Swift Publishing Company. It comes with student workbooks and is designed to teach you or your child how to program using the BASIC language (Beginners All-Purpose Symbolic Instruction Code). This program received the *Learning Magazine* award for Best Microcomputer Software of 1982.

Other excellent programs from this company include *Discover BASIC: Problem Solving with the Apple II Computer* ($74.95) and *The Apple-Based Elementary Mathematics Classroom Learning System* ($495.00). Write for a catalog if you're interested in educational software.

Shelby Lyman Chess Tutorial Series

Krell Software's new series of thirty-nine modules are not for casual chess players. These modules sell for $39.95 each, and are designed to help the serious student of chess improve. Space doesn't permit a complete listing of all thirty-nine modules, but some examples are *The Premature Attack: How to Refute It*, *Exploiting Pawn Weaknesses*, and *The Use of the King in Chess*.

These modules are computer implementations of Socrates Chess Corporation's *Shelby Lyman Chess Tutorial Series*. Lyman is a chess expert and TV commentator and is well known to chess buffs. Most individuals won't be laying out the nearly $1500 for this entire series, but you may want to order just a few of these excellent tutorials to help you with specific parts of your game. We suspect that the main market for this series will be chess clubs and schools.

Hodge Podge

Hodge Podge is just that—a real hodge podge for very young children! The company bills this as an *educational happening* or a *surreptitious learning* program for preschoolers. It's available for $14.95 on cassette or $18.95 on disk from Dynacomp, Inc.

When you press a key, a song, animation, or picture related to the key in some way is heard or appears on the screen. If you press the B key for example, a colorful bear is pictured on the screen with the word BEAR displayed below the graphic. When you press W, a worm crawls across the screen, and if you press Y, *Yankee Doodle* is played and a flag appears on the display.

Logo

In Seymour Papert's book, *Mindstorms*, the author suggests that if educational computing is to be of value, the child must learn to program the computer, rather than the computer programming the child (as in drill and practice programs). Papert is an MIT computer scientist who studied child development for five years in Geneva with the renowned child psychologist, Jean Piaget. Papert and his colleagues then developed Logo, which combines computer capabilities with Piaget's ideas about how children think and learn.

Logo makes it possible for children to actually program the computer to create complex graphics. Children are able to begin doing this after only a five- to ten-minute introduction to Logo commands! Papert believes Logo can actually change the quality of children's thinking. That remains to be proven through research. It is certainly true that children enjoy Logo and learn mathematical and geometric concepts quite easily. We believe Logo holds great promise for educating children, and we recommend its use both at home and at school.

Although Logo will do other things besides create graphics,

many people believe it is the graphics capabilities that are most important for use with children.

Logo graphics revolve around a *turtle*, a triangular object on the screen which can be guided with a series of very simple commands. As the turtle moves, it leaves a line in its path. Complex designs can be created by moving the turtle in this fashion. The child can move the turtle by entering simple commands, one at a time, or a program can be written and run later. There are additional commands that change the background color or the color of the lines drawn by the turtle.

Even if it turns out that Papert is overly optimistic about changing the quality of children's thought, there are other things to recommend Logo. Many children dislike school because they associate it with failure. Logo can give the child successful control of a complex instrument at school. It can motivate the child to learn mathematical and geometric concepts in order to move the turtle efficiently. If errors are made, they are immediately apparent, and the computer is nonjudgmental. This is particularly good if the child is senstitive to adult criticism. Logo can also be used to encourage children to work together as they attempt to solve Logo problems in groups. This can promote cooperation and group problem-solving skills.

There are three very good versions of Logo that will run on your Apple computer. *Apple Logo* is available for $175.00 from Apple Computer Inc. *Krell Logo* is available for $89.95 from Krell Software, and a third Logo, almost identical to Krell's version, is called *Terrapin Logo* ($149.95 from Terrapin Inc.).

A disadvantage of the Logo versions for the Apple is that you cannot create sprites (moving graphics) as you can with Texas Instruments' Logo. Sprite boards and special sprite options are now being marketed for Apple Logo versions, but they are expensive and have some problems. A sprite board for *Terrapin Logo*, for example, sells for $170.00.

If you are interested in purchasing a version of Logo but can't decide which one you should have, we can refer you to a good magazine article. The August 1982 issue of *BYTE* magazine was entirely about Logo. One article by Greg Williams (p. 230) compares and contrasts five versions of Logo. Three of these versions run on the Apple, one is for the TRS-80 Color Computer, and one is the Texas Instruments version. This article can help you decide which version is best for your needs.

Simulations

We have already discussed several simulation programs in the chapter on computer games (Chapter Two). Here are some more.

Eliza

Eliza is a very famous text-only program developed at the Massachusetts Institute of Technology in 1966 by Joseph Weizenbaum, who wrote it as part of MIT's artificial intelligence project. Dr. Weizenbaum is one of the foremost researchers on artificial intelligence. His program responds in a quasi-intelligent fashion to English language questions and statements typed on the computer's keyboard.

The original use of this interesting program was to simulate a psychotherapist talking to a client (the computer is the therapist, you are the client). Weizenbaum reported that the program functioned so realistically that the secreataries in his office eventually requested to be left alone with the computer so they could work out their problems!

The version you can purchase for your Apple is lots of fun and can be used to help learn about artificial intelligence. Here's an excerpt of a conversation with the program that was printed in a recent press release: (*Eliza*'s comments are printed in capital letters)

> Men are all alike.
> IN WHAT WAY?
> They're always bugging us about something or other.

CAN YOU THINK OF A SPECIFIC EXAMPLE?
Well, my boyfriend made me come here.
YOUR BOYFRIEND MADE YOU COME HERE.
THAT'S INTERESTING
He says I'm depressed much of the time.
I AM SORRY TO HEAR YOU ARE DEPRESSED.
It's true. I am unhappy.
DO YOU THINK COMING HERE WILL HELP YOU NOT TO BE UNHAPPY?

The program is available on disk for $25.00 from Artificial Intelligence Research Group.

Isaac Newton and F. G. Newton

These two programs are available on a single disk for $49.95 from Krell Software.

Isaac Newton is an interesting simulation of the use of the scientific method in inquiry. The program generates evidence based on some underlying rule. You may examine the evidence and look for a pattern. The computer then shows you another example and challenges you to say whether this evidence conforms to the underlying rule. Sound complex? Read on.

When you enter the program, you must first decide whether you will play the game alone or with a human opponent, and whether or not you wish *Newton* to select the *Law of Nature* to be used. You will then be asked what level of difficulty you prefer: 1) stranger in a strange land, 2) amateur, 3) lab assistant, 4) junior scientist, 5) master scientist, 6) Magister Ludi, or 7) where angels fear to tread. You must then decide how many correct answers in a row you think you can eventually come up with.

Let's assume that you decide to play against the computer, let the computer select the Law of Nature for the game, choose the easiest level, and decide that you will be able to give five correct answers in a row.

Newton then displays five objects and correctly classifies them for you. The objects are letters and numbers. You can then decide whether you are ready to have *Newton* display another object for you to classify or whether you wish to choose the object and let *Newton* classify it. When you are able to state correctly (five times in a row) whether the object obeys the underlying law of nature as exemplified in the five objects you were shown, you will have achieved a state called *demonstration of knowledge*. That's equivalent to winning.

F. G. Newton is similar, except that it uses graphics. In this one, you are again challenged to discover Newton's laws about objects in the universe, but the objects are square grids. The individual cells in the grid can be filled in or left empty, and you must discover the law determining the pattern.

If this all seems confusing, it's because it is! This is definitely an adult program aimed at teaching logical and analytical thinking and use of the scientific method.

Oil Rig

Oil Rig is a business strategy simulation available for $29.95 from CPU Software. You must buy and sell oil products and drill new wells. Your goal is to become a multi-millionaire and join the Tycoon Club. This is an interesting simulation that uses some arcade-style graphics. Once you decide to drill a well, you use the game paddles to position the rig in such a way that a floating pool of oil will be tapped. The game requires lots of strategy, because you have to keep a lot of variables in mind. This is a fun game that will help you understand our economic system, as well as some aspects of the oil business.

President Elect

President Elect is a political simulation game available for $39.95 from Strategic Simulations.

This is standard political simulation fare. You may choose to manage up to three U.S. presidential candidates. You can choose actual past campaigns, non-historical campaigns, or a hypothetical campaign in 1984. As a game, this program isn't quite fast enough to make the grade and sustain interest. As an educational tool, however, we think it's fine.

Survival Math

Survival Math presents several interesting text-only simulations. It is available for $50.00 from Sunburst Communications. This program is based on the idea that people in many walks of life need some math ability to do their jobs. The four simulations in this package are called Travel Agent Contest, Smart Shopper Marathon, Hot Dog Stand, and Foreman's Assistant. Also included on the disk is a short description of each simulation.

If you choose the Hot Dog Stand program, you are told that your club is planning a hot dog stand at eight home football games. You have $200 to begin with, and your goal is to accumulate $2500. You must purchase hot dogs and buns, chips, soda, napkins, mustard, and relish, and set the price for all items.

The computer determines the weather for the game and decides how many items were sold, calculates your profit and costs, and gives you your new bank balance. You continue until you reach your goal or until you go bankrupt.

This is a very interesting simulation. It could be used to plan for purchasing and setting prices for a real enterprise. It's fun, and you may learn some interesting facts about why you have to pay so much for that hot dog at the next football game you attend.

This software company has some other interesting simulations, so you might want to write and ask for a copy of their catalog.

CHILDREN AND WORD PROCESSING

Children or anyone else who wishes to improve writing or mechanical skills, like grammar, spelling, and punctuation, can profit from word processing. Word processing makes the mechanics of revision easy and encourages you to experiment. Spelling and grammar checkers find errors easily and help you correct your paper without submitting it to the critical eye and red pencil of a teacher.

To benefit the most from word processing, you need to be at least a fairly good typist, so a good typing tutor program is recommended along with a word processing package.

For teaching word processing to children, you can't go wrong with the *Bank Street Writer*, which we review in the chapter on word processing.

MAGAZINES AND BOOKS

Some educational magazines you may be interested in include *Computers in the Schools*, *The Computing Teacher*, and *Educational Computer Magazine*.

Some other magazines that are especially helpful to Apple computer owners are *Apple Orchard*, *Creative Computing*, *NIBBLE*, and *Personal Computing*.

Books of interest include *Computers, Teaching, and Learning* by Willis, Johnson, and Dixon (write for a catalog from dilithium Press) and *The Computer in the School: Tutor, Tool, Tutee* (Columbia University Press, 1981), edited by Robert P. Taylor.

CHAPTER FIVE

Home Finance, Record Keeping, and Health Care

Put Your Apple to Work at Home

Most people don't buy a computer specifically for the uses described in this chapter, but rather for word processing, telecommunications, or playing games. You will probably get a computer for other purposes and then begin looking for more ways to use it. There is a good variety of software for home uses, and we will discuss some of that software here. By watching the ads and reviews in computer magazines, you can become aware of new software as it becomes available.

Interface Age magazine led the way in describing home applications of the microcomputer. Their December 1977 issue has two articles by Francis Ascolillo on a *Household Finance System*. Written in BASIC, the program can give your family an overview of spending and earning patterns. When you write your family checks each month, you simultaneously give the computer the data needed to do an analysis. Monthly and yearly printouts show your spending patterns and predicted trends. The same issue has a personal accounts payable program written in BASIC by Kevin Redden. With it, you can keep track of bills received, payments made, and information like time between receipt and payment, minimum payment due, total amount owed on each account, and interest paid on each account. These BASIC programs can be adapted for your Apple (see Chapter Nine on Programming), or you may purchase similar programs written especially for the Apple.

In addition, many of the popular computer magazines regularly publish programs for the Apple that fall into this category. A well-stocked bookstore will carry at least two or three magazines with listings of software for the Apple.

THE APPLE AS A HOME FINANCIAL MANAGER

A growing number of programs help home computer owners make personal financial decisions. These programs can help you control your budget, do financial planning, balance your checkbook, analyze your loan options, and file your income tax.

Q-PON Helper

Do you save cash-off product coupons? If so, and if you're like most coupon savers, you probably have a big problem keeping track of your coupons. You just can't remember whether or not you have a coupon good for fifty cents off a box of Soggysweet Cereal. The only thing you can find is a coupon good for half off a five-color *Don't Mess With Me* tattoo at the Happy Sailor tattoo parlor! Then just when you've decided to settle for the tattoo, you discover the coupon expired seven years ago! Finding the right coupon can be a real hassle. You might even be one of those people who would like to save money with coupons, but you haven't bothered because of the problem of getting organized.

Q-PON Helper (disk—$19.75 from LAST) is designed to help you avoid such problems. You can keep a well-organized, up-to-date list of up to 300 coupons. Anytime you want, you can get a display of all information about all coupons in your collection. Or you can elect to search your file for coupons good on items costing more than a given amount, for all coupons for dairy products, and so on.

You can also get a display of all coupons worth more than an amount you specify. That should be handy on double stamp day at your local market. Another option is to display information on all coupons due to expire on a given date. By displaying all coupons on products with a certain brand name, you can quickly find out if you have a coupon good for products you buy on a regular basis, such as Sumptuous Brand Candied Ants, or the like.

This is a very useful program and should prove to be invaluable for anyone who saves coupons.

Tax Break Annual and **Tax Break Planner**

The purpose of these two programs is a noble one: to make sure you don't pay a penny more in income taxes than you actually owe! They are typical of the income tax software currently available for your Apple computer. *Tax Break Annual* is designed to help you save money and prepare your income tax for a given year. *Tax Break Planner* will do the same thing, but will also help you analyze, project, and keep your hypothetical tax payments as low as possible for the next three years.

Tax Break Annual sells for $129.95 and *Tax Break Planner* is $179.95. Both are available from Proforma Software.

Either of these programs can be used to verify addition, subtraction and table lookup values before you mail your return to the IRS. This way you can make certain you have taken all tax benefits you are entitled to, red-flag any deductions that may be challenged, and determine if you should use the five-year income averaging schedule. These programs have many other features designed to be of help for tax returns with a wide variety of problems.

This is sophisticated tax software that can be used to do everything except actually type in the values on your return.

Figure 5.1 Tax Break Planner

It is as simple to use as such a complex program can be. It is menu-driven, and the prompts are clearly stated and easy to understand.

Money Street

Money Street is a checkbook financial system that can end those out-of-balance blues forever. It is available for $99.95 from Computer Tax Service.

Money Street is actually three programs with many uses. One is a checkbook manager, one is an accounting system, and the third is a financial information system. You can sort checks into 100 business, personal, or tax categories by month, payee, deposits, code number, uncleared items, checkbook history, amount, and by many other variables. You can print fifteen different reports of expenses, income, and profit by month or by year-to-date. You can find a cancelled check in one minute—even in a file of 1000 checks. For tax purposes,

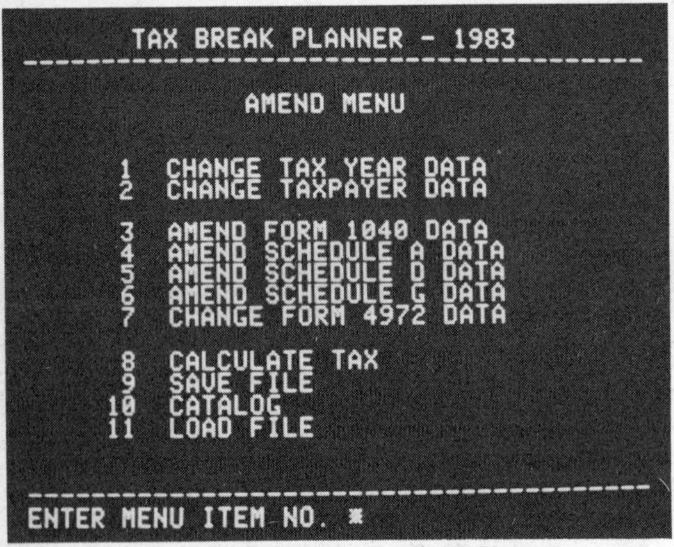

Figure 5.2 Menu from Tax Break Planner

you can get a printout of income and deductions that is up-to-the minute and accurate.

Money Street will handle as many checking accounts as you please, but you have to use a separate data disk for each account. You can set it up to work for fiscal or calendar years, and there is a roll-over feature at year's end.

Money Street creates an electronic facsimile of your checkbook on the computer screen. You see seventeen items at one time. For each transaction, the screen displays number, month, day, payee, code number, and amount. A running balance at the bottom of the screen lets you confirm arithmetic. When you are ready to balance your checkbook, you simply enter the numbers of all checks that have cleared, and the program does the rest. After you enter the number and press ENTER, the program displays all the information for that check, then prompts for the next number. Again, the line at the bottom of the screen keeps a running total.

The program gives you 100 codes. You name these codes as you please. You can then sort your files based on any of these codes. This can be great for income tax, for example. If you code 81 as the number for unreimbursed business expenses, you'll have the total at your fingertips at tax time. You can get an itemized printout of these expenses at any time.

This is an extremely good program for checkbook management. It is very flexible and has many sophisticated features. Most of all, this program is very easy to learn and to use.

Amort

Amort is a typical loan analysis program. It will give you amortization data and a complete loan analysis. It will also figure compound and present value of an annuity. It is available for $22.95 from Garbo Software.

The Family Budget

The Family Budget, available for $34.95 from Dynacomp, Inc., is designed to help you keep track of the money you spend each year. There are two parts to this program. Part One is used to record all money paid out each day over a one-year period. There are twenty-eight categories for coding transactions, plus three categories for tax-deductible expenditures. Part Two is used to record all credit transactions. You can get a printout from either part at any time.

USING YOUR APPLE COMPUTER FOR RECORD-KEEPING AT HOME

You can keep records of many things at home with your microcomputer. You can buy software for everything from keeping track of recipes to storing bartending instructions.

Apple Disk Librarian

One program that helps you keep track of the programs stored on your disks is called *Apple Disk Librarian*. This is a good free disk-organizing system, written by George D. Parker and printed in *NIBBLE* magazine, Vol. 4, No. 1, 1983, p. 13. *Apple Disk Librarian* is a cataloging system for DOS 3.3 disks that can really bring order into your computing life. If you have only ten or fifteen disks, keeping track of which disk holds what is probably no problem. But if home computing has become important to you, it won't be long before you have fifty or more disks, and that's when you'll need a disk catalog.

Apple Disk Librarian helps you to number your disks (up to 500 of them). The program writes the number into a file and catalogs the contents of each one. You can then use the program to find a file, to determine what files are on any one diskette, or to print a list of all or some of your files.

This is a very helpful program for anyone who is beginning to accumulate lots of disks. The program is quite lengthy for a type-it-yourself program. If you aren't interested in doing that, there is an alternative. Most magazines that print entire programs also sell those programs on disks. *NIBBLE* is no exception. Most of their diskettes cost about $20 and contain from two to five programs. If you're interested, write *NIBBLE*.

Magic Memory

Magic Memory is a personal record-keeping system available from ARTSCI, Inc., on diskette for $99.95. This computer-based filing system is designed to be used by people with very little computer experience. It helps you set up a database of any kind of information.

The displays are designed to resemble a traditional paper-and-pencil notebook with alphabetized paper tabs. The letters from A through Z are listed down the right side of the screen. You select one of these by moving the cursor on top of it and pressing ENTER. This *opens the book*. Other tabs are available, which you can label as you choose. For example, you might label one *orchids*, one *daisies*, and one *rhododendrons*.

The program gives you a fast, easy way to create, maintain, and use your own customized files. Because it's a general record-keeper, you can tailor it to fit your own needs. It can be used for recipes, tax records, shopping lists, Christmas card lists, and for many other purposes.

Micro Cookbook

This cookbook program is available from Virtual Combinatics for $40.00. *Micro Cookbook* is actually far more than a cookbook. Oh sure, it includes more than 200 international recipes, and there are already two add-on disks available with specialized recipes (*Appetizers* and *Soups and Salads*, $12 each). But the program itself is what makes *Micro Cookbook* special.

First of all, it's quite easy to use. One reason is that it's completely menu-driven (what else would a cookbook program be?). Not only is it easy to use, but you can do so much with it! You can add all your own favorite recipes. You can tell the cookbook how many are coming for dinner, and it will automatically adjust the ingredient amounts. You can tell the program what ingredients you have in the house, and the program will tell you which recipes you can prepare. You can display nutrition and calorie guides and a glossary of cooking terms. You can even print a shopping list by telling the program what meals you have in mind for the week.

Apple Tree Genealogy System

Designed to help you plot your family tree, this program is available from J. Fiske Software Systems, Inc. You can enter up to 1000 names and keep a cross-indexed record of family relationships. If you're into genealogy, this program is a must!

USING YOUR COMPUTER FOR HOME HEALTH CARE

Home health care is a promising new area for home computer use. Although there isn't a great deal of software available in this area, we expect the future to bring increased interest and, consequently, much more software related to home health care.

NODVILL Diet Program

This handy diet program is available on disk for $69.95 from NODVILL Software. It will help you be sure you're eating healthfully and will help you plan nutritious meals.

One of the first things you must do is determine your approximate energy expenditure and enter it in the program. The manual lists a variety of activities under the low, medium, and high energy levels. For example, lying down or sleeping is a low energy activity that burns off only about eighty calories per hour. Running is a high energy activity that requires about 900 calories per hour. (There are no statistics listed for compulsive computing.) The program also prompts you for less interesting but more objective data, such as name, age, weight, and height. The program then shows you what your nutritional requirements are in terms of units of vitamins and minerals.

There is a subprogram that helps you enter the types of food you like. It displays the nutritional content of the food, including how many calories it contains. There are over 700 foods included, and you can add the data for sauteed hummingbird wings or other personal favorites not included in the program. Another subprogram helps you plan meals for a seven-day period, and another uses the menus you have generated to print out a shopping list to take to the supermarket.

Medical Adviser

Medical Adviser is an attempt to provide some simple medical diagnoses at home. It's available for $37.50 from Navic Corporation.

The computer asks a series of questions regarding symptoms. You type in your answers. *Medical Adviser* then attempts to identify a disease or condition that fits your unique pattern of answers. About 200 illnesses are catalogued.

This program could be beneficial in providing some needed health information, but we think you should be careful about over-reliance on the program.

Psychological Self-Analysis

These five programs are available for $24.99 from Huntington Computing. They are intended, logically enough, to give you some insight into your own psychological make-up. Nine multiple-choice tests are included on this disk. The results are used to assess assertiveness, conscience, manipulation, marital adjustment, personal adjustment, preferred activities, sexual attitudes, and individual scale of values.

Executive Fitness

This interesting exercise program is available for $19.95 from Monument Computer Service. You type in your age and other statistics, and the program prescribes an exercise program you can perform indoors. Graphics demonstrate the exercises and set the tempo. The exercises increase in difficulty until you have reached the ideal fitness level for your age.

32 BASIC Programs for the Apple Computer

This especially good software bargain is available for $34.95 from dilithium Software. *32 BASIC Programs* comes with a full-length book by Tom Rugg and Phil Feldman, as well as a diskette containing the thirty-two programs. The package includes educational, graphics, and math programs, as well as games and programs for home use.

Some of the home programs are *Biorhythm*, *Checkbook*, *Loan*, and *Mileage*. The uses for those programs are obvious from their names. The package also includes *Decide*, a unique program designed to help you make decisions involving the selection of one alternative from several choices. It works by prying relevant information from you and then organizing it in a meaningful, quantitative manner. Your best choice will be indicated and all of the possibilities given a relative rating.

You can use *Decide* for a wide variety of decisions. It can help with things like choosing the best stereo system, saying yes or no to a job or business offer, or selecting the best course of action for the future. Everything is personalized to your individual decision.

The unique thing about this package is the documentation. Since all thirty-two programs are listed in their entirety, it is extremely easy to revise them if you haye the ability and are so inclined. If not, the book does a great job of teaching you to use them as-is.

CHAPTER SIX

Tapping into the World: Telecommunications

Imagine touching a few keys on your Apple IIe computer and making all your travel arrangements yourself at any hour of the day or night. How about being able to read the latest newswire or stock report at the same time the editor of your newspaper does? How would you like to read movie reviews or pro-football statistics on your computer screen? How about the excitement of immediately announcing a new baby to your friends all over the country by typing a few words? These are some of the things you can do with telecommunications.

You already know about the video game potential of personal computers. You also know that those desktop marvels playing *Apple Panic*, *Frogger*, and *Deadline* can do an honest day's work as word processors, accounting machines, and educational tools. The subject of this chapter is not so well known, however. Telecomputing involves connecting your home computer to other computers over standard phone lines. Your computer becomes a link to hundreds, perhaps thousands, of other computers that have been programmed to provide various services. You can sit back in your easy chair, get a comfortable grip on the Apple IIe's keyboard, and do everything from pay bills to read weather reports for Colorado ski resorts.

Telecomputing is, in fact, one of the fastest growing areas

of personal computer use. Many Apple IIe owners regularly use their computer to talk to other computers. You need three things for telecomputing: a computer, a special device called a *modem*, and a phone line. You dial another computer's number and, when it answers, you talk to the computer by typing on the keyboard of the Apple IIe. The computer on the other end of the phone line responds to your requests by transmitting information that is displayed on your television or monitor screen.

Because most people may not be familiar with telecommunications, we have included a somewhat extended introduction to the topic in this chapter. We'll explain the concept of telecommunications, then give you some general examples of how it can be used. We will tell you about the different kinds of information you can get. Then there are some specific examples of services available to Apple IIe owners, and we'll tell you exactly what equipment and software you need to get started.

Telecommunications are complicated. There are many aspects of the phenomenon and many ways the home computer owner can take advantage of the services available. Explaining it is a little like trying to explain reading and talking. The skills of reading and talking are really *tools*. If you have them, you can do many different things, like read the morning paper or decode the assembly instructions that came with your son's Christmas bicycle. The ability to telecommunicate also gives you many ways to acquire and use information. Over the last century the development of wireless communication technology such as radio, television, and satellite transmission systems changed the way we get much of our information. It also changed the type of information we get. If you have cable television, for example, you can tune to an all-news channel and get instant information on current news stories. Cable channels give you specific types of information in areas such as health and nutrition and business news.

Cable-based information systems all share one problem, however. You are a passive viewer with no direct control over the material you view. Yes, you can tune to the health and nutrition news channel, but it may or may not do a piece on the particular topic you want to hear about. Telecommunications will let you take a much more active role in the selection of information.

MAJOR TELECOMMUNICATIONS APPLICATIONS FOR HOME COMPUTERS

What are Information Utilities?

When you go to your kitchen sink to get a glass of water, you simply turn on the tap, and out flows the water. The water comes from some large reservoir of water stored at some distant location. A similar thing happens when you turn on the electric lights in your home or when you tune into your favorite cable television station. Water, electricity, and cable television services are called *utilities*. A utility service becomes available to you when you have the proper receiving equipment—the kitchen sink, the electric light, or the television set—and when the receiving equipment is properly connected and the utility bill all paid up.

Telecommunications can be thought of as a large family of *information utilities* that can be brought into your home or office through your personal computer. We will use the term information utilities in a very broad sense to include any source of information that can be accessed by a computer through telecommunications. Some computer writers use this term to describe only the very large systems that offer a wide variety of services. We like to think of an information utility as any kind of information service, large or small, local or national. In other words, anyone offering information that can be received by a personal computer over the telephone lines is an information utility.

Starting with this definition of an information utility, we

can say that lots of information utilities are now in operation, and many more will come on line in the near future. To receive such a service, you will need the right equipment and the appropriate connections. In most cases, you will need to pay a utility fee, but some of these services are free. More detail will be given later on how all this works. For now let's look at some of the many utility services available for your computer.

Local Area Networks and Computer Bulletin Boards

There are hundreds of local computer *networks* now operating in this country. Most use regular phone lines for communications. They're run by universities and colleges, computer clubs, amateur radio clubs, and special interest groups. Members of the sponsoring organization (or, in some cases, anyone who knows the phone number) interact with the network's computer. Some systems limit use to reading the local electronic bulletin board; others let you use a large computer system's power from your own home.

A typical local area network will be sponsored by a computer club, which pays for a phone line connected to a computer owned by the club. When you call, the computer answers the phone electronically and asks what information you would like to have transmitted to your computer. There may be options such as reading the latest issue of the club's newsletter, browsing through want ads for used equipment, or looking at material written by other Apple IIe owners about new products or problems. The type of network and the services offered vary greatly from one locale to the other. Local computer stores and computer clubs are usually aware of the networks operating in the area and what they offer. Many local networks are the electronic equivalent of the bulletin board down at the laundromat or at the factory, with notices of events, want ads, offers of free puppies or kittens, and descriptions of new computer equipment.

National Networks and Bulletin Boards

In addition to local computer bulletin boards, several national systems (some with toll-free numbers) are available for the cost of the phone call. National bulletin boards are generally intended for a special audience, and some charge for their use. HEX (Handicapped Education Exchange), reached by dialing (301) 593–7033, is used by individuals and organizations to exchange information on how technology can be used to help the handicapped. There are also national networks for owners of a particular brand of computer. Some of the Apple networks will be described in a later section of this chapter.

If you would like to get information on all computer bulletin board systems (CBBS) there is, appropriately enough, an electronic way to do it. Novation, one of the larger manufacturers of modems, has a bulletin board of its own. It provides information on the hundreds of free CBBSs across the country. When you have your Apple IIe set up for telecomputing, you can dial (213) 881–6880. When Novation's computer answers the phone, you will probably need to hit the RETURN key once or twice, and Novation should respond with:

LOGON PLEASE

Most networks require you to sign on. In this case, all you need to do is type CAT (Novation makes CAT modems) and press RETURN. You are then given access to this CBBS. It has a list of hundreds of other CBBSs, organized by area code. The system also has many other services, such as games you can play (remember that the call is long distance for most people and could get expensive).

Recreational Games

Both CompuServe and The Source, telecomputing department stores that are discussed later in this chapter, have provisions for playing games. Dial their numbers, type in your personal identification code, then play any of over 100 different games. Most games are the adventure or strategy type with little or no graphics, because it is difficult to transmit graphics quickly over phone lines and virtually impossible, without lots of specialized software, to transmit usable graphics to all the different models of personal computers on the market today.

Downloading Programs

Several networks sell programs by *downloading* them to your computer and billing the cost to a credit card. Some services even let you try the program first. If you like it, the program is yours for a small fee. Before you can download programs, you must buy a special program that lets you store the programs you buy on a cassette or disk.

Databases

A database is simply a batch of information stored in the memory of a computer. If you need to know the current price of Apple stock or the time of the next plane to Lubbock, this information—and much more—is available from databases that make up one of the many information utilities. Both The Source and CompuServe have such information stored in extensive databases. A doctor can check on a recommended treatment for a new disease, a farmer can get predictions on the wheat crop in South America, a consumer can check discount prices on a dishwasher or color television.

Some writers predict that these large computerized information utilities, with their huge databases, will replace traditional sources of news and information, such as newspapers and television newscasts. We doubt that. Newspapers are sources of professionally packaged and conveniently presented general information. We think information utilities are likely to be added to our existing sources of information rather than replacing them.

The reason is the fact that information utilities are not easy to access; it takes some effort to get information from them. In addition, they are not very convenient sources of general information. The morning paper or the nightly news gives us that. What information utilities do best is provide us with access to specific information.

Suppose you are a member of a local group formed to fight for modifications in local laws governing waste disposal near the subdivision where you live. One task the group must accomplish is to write a booklet, which will be distributed to citizens and local officials. You want the booklet to be technically accurate, and you want to include information on what has happened in other areas that faced a similar problem.

It would be possible to gather the background and support information you need by going to the library and searching through the relevant indexes for articles and books on the topic. A hand search would probably take a day or two of hard work at the library and probably wouldn't be as comprehensive as it should. An alternative is a computerized search through one of the databases from an information utility called DIALOG (described later). A DIALOG search will provide you with a list of articles (with abstracts or summaries of the articles) and books on the topic. A DIALOG search would take less than an hour and would be more comprehensive. But even a DIALOG search is unlikely to point you to recent news stories on the topic. Those can be accessed through one of the general information utilities, like The Source or CompuServe. What do you do if you want a summary of all the federal court cases relevant to this particular type of pollution? There is a database that will provide that for you. A database may contain millions of references to books, articles, and technical papers. It can be searched electronically by telling the computer to look for references with information about a particular topic. By using a computer to find the information, the time is reduced, and the quality of the search is improved.

There are hundreds of databases available through information utilities today that are of interest to professionals in virtually every field. You can use your Apple IIe to find information on new metallurgical patents, federal court cases, space games, college scholarships, and much more.

Banking and Shopping

Several banks, led by the United American Bank of Knoxville, have systems that let customers transfer funds and pay bills by computer. Dial the bank's number, type in your account number, then type in the instructions on how much to pay whom. Chemical Bank of New York even has provisions for making purchases like airline tickets, which are mailed to you and debited to your account. Some experts foresee banking by computer as a commonplace activity in the future. At present it is limited to a few areas where it is being test-marketed and to people who use information utilities like CompuServe that have banking facilities.

Shopping by computer has caught the public's eye. Several shopping services let you order items, which are charged to your credit card and mailed to your home or office. Both The Source and CompuServe have shopping services. In addition, many services provide consumer information of various types, for example, movie and book reviews.

Electronic Mail and Teleconferencing

Electronic mail means different things to different people. A large corporation may have computers that store messages written in the Dallas office to staff in the Chicago office. Late at night the Dallas computer automatically calls up the Chicago computer and transmits the messages. When the recipient of a message arrives at work the next day, a flashing light on a desktop computer console indicates there is a message waiting in the computer's memory. That is electronic mail.

Public access electronic mail involves typing a message in on your keyboard. Your message is sent to a company that handles electronic mail. It transmits the message to the city where the recipient lives. The message may then be printed out and delivered by the Post Office the next day. In the future, the recipient may have a home computer that is always connected to the phone line. Messages may be transmitted directly to the home and printed out by a printer attached to the computer.

Today a form of electronic mail is possible through the information utilities. Each person who has an account with a utility like The Source has a user number. That number serves as an electronic address. If you need to send a report to a friend or co-worker who lives across the country, you can transmit the report (which you typed on a word processor) from your computer to The Source. When your friend next uses The Source, it indicates a message is waiting. The report would then be transmitted from The Source to your friend, who could transfer it from the computer's memory to a disk or cassette.

MAJOR INFORMATION UTILITIES

Currently there are two established national general-purpose information utilities: The Source and CompuServe. Both can be used by anyone with a small computer, a credit card (so they can bill you), and a telephone. Calls to the two major systems are local in many major cities. You are connected to them through special electronic communication networks—usually Telenet or Tymnet.

The Source

The Source is a service of Source Telecomputing Corporation. If you want to sign up, you can do so through the mail or at many computer stores. As with cable television, there is an initial hookup charge ($100). After that, The Source charges $7.75 per hour during non-business hours, less for late night use, $5.75, and during office hours, $20.75 an hour. There is a minimum monthly charge of $10, whether you use the system or not. The phone call to The Source is a local one in over 300 cities.

Few people will use every service offered by The Source, now a subsidiary of Reader's Digest, but it's nice to know they're there. Here are some of the most interesting services:

• *Electronic Mail.* In addition to the method of electronic mail described earlier, it is possible to dial a toll-free number and dictate a letter over the phone. Your letter is put in the electronic mail file and is available to the recipient the next time that person signs on. Special interest groups can also use the electronic mail feature by placing information in a sort of electronic bulletin board, which can be read by subscribers with similar interests. There is also an electronic equivalent of junk mail. You can type in a letter or report and tell the system to send it to as many Source subscribers as you wish.

• *Electronic Travel Service.* In addition to being able to make your own airline and hotel reservations, you can get restaurant rating guides and international airline schedules. You have access to worldwide airline flight information, which is updated every two weeks. If you are going to visit either New York or Washington, D.C., you can get listings of services ranging all the way from fur rental to babysitting. One part of this service, called the Travel Club, can be used just like a travel agency. You can wrap up all of your travel plans by asking the Travel Club to order tickets and make reservations.

• *Education.* The Source has quite a few drill and practice programs on a variety of topics suitable for both children and adults. You can call on these programs to help your children learn how to count, learn the alphabet, learn the decimal system, and much more. Programs to teach spelling, math, foreign languages and science are available. In addition, there is a directory of financial support possibilities for college students and a job service that lets you type in your resume so prospective employers can review it. There is also a jobs-available listing.

• *Consumer Aids.* You can read informative articles on how to reduce energy costs and save gasoline. You can get assistance in choosing the right wines or vitamins. One part of this service, called *Comp-U-Store*, amounts to an electronic supermarket. You can review items and prices on the computer screen and place your order from the computer's keyboard. Then there is *TradeNet*, a barter service. With it, you can barter trips, professional advice on a range of subjects, and items of almost any description. The service also has restaurant guides and reviews for most large cities, and a movie review section.

• *Sports News*. Up-to-the-minute news on sports, team standings, sports trivia and sports records are available. Round-ups of scores on a national, international, and statewide level are available.

• *Financial Service*. Business and financial forecasts from professional economists and security analysts are up-dated weekly.

• *Portfolio Management*. You have access to a system that will help you create and maintain your personal investment portfolio. When you enter a file name that contains your stocks, you'll receive an up-to-date report on each stock on your computer screen.

• *Legi-Slate*. You can track bills referred out of Congressional committees and list members of Congress by state, party, committee, and subcommittee. This service is up-dated weekly.

• *Commodity News Service, Inc*. You can use this service to track price movements in commodities futures markets. You can also read market commentary and commodity news.

• *Computing Services*. You can write and run programs in a variety of languages including BASIC, COBOL, Pascal, and FORTRAN, among others. The Source also makes available quite a few canned programs of their own. Many are free; some involve a small extra charge. These programs include games, business software, and software for special applications like statistical analysis of large amounts of data. You cannot buy these programs and run them without being connected to the service. In essence, you *rent* them by connecting to The Source by phone and typing in the name of the program you want to use.

• *Databases*. A service likely to be used by many subscribers is access to some of the many databases available from The Source. One of the more popular databases is the United Press International (UPI) wire service. It is possible to tell The Source to put the UPI output on the screen and watch the news scroll by a line at a time. However, that is a very inefficient way of finding the news you're interested in. From your computer you can tell the UPI database exactly which stories you want to read. If you want information on the latest crisis in any country, you can type in the name of the country, and all the recent stories filed with UPI about that country will be displayed. It is easy to get in-depth reports on any subject you are interested in. Best of all, you can have up-to-date information any time you want it. The UPI database is only one of a large number of databases available on The Source. It takes some effort to learn how to use them effectively, but the effort is well worth it.

Many of the databases are oriented toward a particular topic. If you are interested in the stock market, for example, you can get detailed news and background information relevant to specific companies. There are databases on commodities, stocks, bonds, precious metals, and more. There is an electronic version of the magazine *U.S. News and World Report*, as well as abstracts of articles from magazines like *Forbes* and *Harvard Business Review*.

CompuServe

The major competitor to The Source is CompuServe Information Service, now a subsidiary of H & R Block. There are many similarities between the two major information utilities and some differences. CompuServe has an initiation fee of around $30 and charges $5 per hour during non-business hours. CompuServe is not available during normal working hours, since the company that runs this service uses its computers to serve commercial customers during that time. The connect call is a local one in over 300 cities.

CompuServe offers services similar to those of The Source. Instead of UPI, CompuServe uses the Associated Press newswire, and it has electronic editions of papers such as the *St. Louis Post-Dispatch*. There are also electronic editions of popular magazines like *Computers and Electronics*, *Better Homes and Gardens*, and *Popular Science*. CompuServe also has a newsletter for Apple computer owners. A tremendous amount of information is available on Apple computers, with a special section devoted to the Apple IIe. This is one way to get up-to-date information on these computers.

CompuServe also offers information on topics as diverse as home repair, personal health, and recipes. Like The Source, it has book and movie reviews, as well as a sports information service. There is even a file of computer art that can be copied on your printer.

Like The Source, CompuServe has a number of financial databases you can use to investigate and track the performance of stock and commodities. There is also a way of banking electronically on CompuServe through a bank in Boston. The service also has an electronically searchable version of the *World Book Encyclopedia*, a program that helps you select a college, and a service called *Refundle Bundle* for coupon clippers.

CompuServe sign-up kits are available from several sources, including many computer stores and CompuServe. The base fee is $20, but most people buy at least $10 worth of manuals to help them learn how to use CompuServe. A CompuServe Starter Kit, which includes manuals and several hours of time, is $40.

Both CompuServe and The Source add new services regularly, and both offer value for the money you pay.

OTHER INFORMATION UTILITIES

In addition to the general-purpose information supermarkets, there are many specialized systems that offer a more limited range of services. What they lack in breadth is more than offset by their depth.

Bulletin Boards for the Apple

Many specialized bulletin boards are available for Apple computer owners. The June 1983 issue of *inCider* magazine lists several, in an article called "Worlds of Communication," by Peter Ferrand and John Davidson.

When you use these bulletin board services, you can download programs from them. Don't expect to find a $200 piece of software that you can download free, however. Most of the programs you get from these services were written by nonprofessionals, and they are not guaranteed to run perfectly. There will be some good ones, and the only cost to you is the long distance telephone service you use while the program is downloading.

One problem with small, specialized bulletin boards is that they are often short-lived. Someone may start a good bulletin board and run it for several months, and then, for one reason or another, drop it. The best way to keep up on bulletin boards is to watch for listings in the computer magazines. In the case of the Apple IIe, you should especially watch *Apple Orchard*, *NIBBLE*, and *inCider*.

Knowledge Index

This service is a special microcomputer version of DIALOG Information Service. DIALOG has a huge computer complex containing billions of references on every imaginable subject. Because of the high cost of the DIALOG service, it is used primarily by professionals at libraries and universities. You use it if you are trying to get information on a specialized topic. Instead of going to the library and searching through references, books, and magazines, the computer does all of the searching and gathers the information for you. *Knowledge Index* costs $35 for the initial sign-up. With this initial fee, you get two hours of search time. After that, it will cost $24 an hour to use the system.

Dow Jones News/Retrieval Service

You can join this service for an initial fee of $50. There is no monthly fee, but you are charged for the time you use the system. This charge varies, depending on which part of the service you are using. As you might expect, this service deals with the stock market. In Chapter Eight, there is description of a special program that you will want to use with this service.

Money DOS

This service is free, and you can access it by dialing the telephone number once you are set up for telecommunications with the Apple IIc computer. Money DOS is a bulletin board on financial investments. The person who gives the advice and runs thc bullctin board is J. M. Keynes, who is senior vice president of investments for a member firm of the New York Stock Exchange.

The Encyclopaedia Britannica

This gives you the full text of the *Britannica 3* encyclopedia and covers the ten-volume *Micropedia*, which contains important facts in capsule form. Other special editions such as *Book of the Year* are also included.

GETTING ON LINE

Does one or more of the possibilities in telecommunications arouse your interest? Would you like to use your Apple IIe to connect yourself to a bulletin board or information utility?

Connecting the Apple II to a Modem

Your Apple IIe computer does not automatically come ready to be connected to a modem. There are two common ways to get it connected. One way is to buy a modem that inserts directly into an Apple expansion slot located in the back of the computer. You can see the slots by simply lifting the cover off the computer. The other way is to buy an RS-232 card and a regular modem. The RS-232 card also fits into an expansion slot in the computer. You then connect the computer to the modem with a cable that attaches to the RS-232 card.

RS-232 cards cost between $75 and $190 and can be purchased at your local Apple dealer. These cards are also sold by third-party dealers, and you can probably get them cheaper if you shop around.

Modems

A modem converts the electronic signals used inside your computer into signals that can be sent over the telephone lines. It also translates the sounds sent to you over the telephone line into electronic signals your computer can use. A modem hooks the telephone line to your computer. Modems with several different features are available for the Apple IIe computer. These features have to do with how the modem hooks to your computer as well as how it hooks to the telephone line. There are also some special features that make it possible for you to gain automatic access to an information source. Like nearly all other computer accessories, modems are available in a wide range of options and prices.

The two most common modems that insert directly into the expansion slots of the Apple IIe are:

- *The Hayes Micromodem II*. This is a complete telecommunications package. It consists of a modem on an expansion card that plugs into a slot in the computer, all of the necessary cables to connect it to the telephone line, and a complete instruction manual. You also receive a disk that contains examples of how the package can be used. This package by Hayes Microcomputer Products is $379. This is a sophisticated modem with many extra features.

• *Apple Cat II*. This modem system is similar to *The Hayes Micromodem*. The *Apple Cat II* will accept and send information at a faster transmission rate, but the faster rate cannot be used on many of the most popular networks. This modem sells for $389.

When it comes to external modems that will connect to a RS-232 card, there are many different makes and models to choose from. Several that are popular among Apple IIe owners are listed below:

• Hayes Microcomputer Products, the manufacturer of the *Micromodem II*, also makes a modem called the *Smartmodem*. The *Smartmodem* connects to an RS-232 card and then into the telephone line. This modem can automatically dial a number and answer the phone. It has gained great popularity with Apple owners due to its ease of use. This modem costs $289.

• The *212A/D Modem*, sold by Universal Data Systems, has a built-in program that lets you store up to nine thirty-digit numbers. They could be the telephone numbers and access codes for an information utility. When the numbers have been stored, you can call up the number and tell the computer to log you on to the information utility. This modem has most of the extras you will ever need. It is a very expensive model, retailing for $795.

• If you don't want to spend very much money and don't mind using a plain, no-frills modem, you might consider the *Signalman Modem* for $79 from Computer Exchange.

Software for Telecommunications

A critical portion of your telecommunications system is a software package that will tell the Apple IIe computer how to send and receive information. A variety of inexpensive terminal packages are available for Apple computers, some priced as low as $30. You also get software free with most of the modems designed specifically for the Apple IIe. A reliable product in this category is *VisiTerm* sold by VisiCorp. This terminal software package sells for $129 and has all the standard features and many others.

There is also a variety of more expensive software packages. One of the most flexible programs is *Transend* 1,2, and 3 from Microcomputer Products. There are three versions of this package. Version 1 is the no-frills version, and version 3 is the Mercedes-Benz. All three of the Transend programs turn the Apple IIe into a very smart telecommunications computer. Version 1 costs $89, version 2 costs $149, and version 3 costs $275.

THE FUTURE OF TELECOMMUNICATIONS

As with many other computer applications, we are only beginning to see what can be done. As the information utility services expand to offer more and better services, your Apple IIe will become a more useful tool. One computer enthusiast predicts that in a few years, communications programs will be fully integrated with other programs under a master operating system. Establishing a telephone connection and exchanging files will be one simple integrated function. It will be exciting to see what the future holds.

CHAPTER SEVEN

Word Processing

WHAT IS WORD PROCESSING?

When you think of a computer, you may think of numbers, numbers, and more numbers. Are computers *number crunchers*, machines capable of performing thousands of calculations a second? Yes, they are, and the next chapter on business and professional applications deals with the ability of the computer to manipulate and massage all sorts of numbers for you.

Computers are also for word people. We feel, in fact, that computers, particularly personal computers, may well turn out to do more work with words than with numbers. The chapter on telecommunications shows you how to harness the power of the computer to acquire and communicate information. That is called *information processing*. This chapter focuses on the role of the computer in helping you create written documents—from a quick note for the folks back East to that great American novel you always wanted to write. Using a computer to help you write your own material is called *word processing*.

In the past eight years we have used word processors exclusively to write and edit over twenty books about computers and related topics. That experience, you would think, should give us an excellent perspective from which to evaluate the relative merits of the Apple IIe as a word processor and to critique word processing programs. There is a problem with the perspective we have. We probably use our computers an average of eight to ten hours a day, day after day, for word processing, which places rigorous demands on the machine and the software. Although we did not use the Apple IIe to write this book, it can be a very good word processing system for both home and office use. It has some limitations. All computers today do, but the Apple is not a good choice for people who plan to do a lot of word processing on their computer unless you spend some money on optional hardware.

WHY USE A WORD PROCESSOR?

If you are an accomplished typist and own a typewriter, why should you learn to use a word processor? If you type documents that are used only once, and you always type them perfectly, there is little reason to learn word processing. If you make errors, if you find yourself typing the same thing several times (for example, a letter to be mailed to several people), or if you must regularly revise and retype documents, a word processor can help you do more work in less time.

A friend of ours is the chairman of a scholarship committee that awards eight college scholarships each year and receives between 50 and 150 applications. Each year he must send out eight letters congratulating those who received the awards, eight letters to the alternates who might still get the award if some of the first eight decide not to attend college, and a larger number of letters to the people who were turned down. He has three standard letters that he modifies slightly each year. Before he began using the word processor, he or his secretary had to type each letter, check it for errors, retype it if errors were found, and finally sign and mail each one. With a word processor, he tells the program to load the file containing the sample letter into the computer's memory, the computer displays the letter on the screen, and he edits it to reflect circumstances related to the current year's competition, adding any personal messages he wants. Then he types the correct address at the top of the letter (actually at the top of the screen) and presses the keys to tell the computer to print out a copy on a *letter quality* printer, one with print that looks as good as that produced by a standard office typewriter.

Once the current version of the letter is in the computer's memory, he need only add the address, salutation, and individual comments. If eighty percent of the letter remains the same, that part need not be retyped for each person who receives the letter. So he doesn't waste time typing the same thing over and over, or increase the likelihood of making a new error when he retypes material that has already been typed correctly.

As our friend adds comments and the address to the standard letter, he occasionally makes a mistake. On a typewriter he would have to stop and correct the error. If the typewriter is a self correcting model, he might be able to make the correction cleanly and quickly. But if he leaves out a line or wants to add a word in the middle of a sentence, he would have to retype the entire letter.

With virtually all word processing programs you can *insert* and *delete* material electronically. If you typed *Tkhis* when you wanted *This*, it is easy to use the cursor control keys (the ones with the arrows on them) to move the cursor over the top of the *k* in *Tkhis*. Press the DEL key, and the *k* disappears. In addition, the word processor fills in the space. Instead of *T his* you have *This*. Most word processors let you delete material a character at a time, and some allow deletion of words, sentences, even paragraphs by pressing one or two keys. The insert function works much like the delete function. If you type *Your application was one of the best* and then decide that you want to add the word *very* after *the*, it is a simple matter for a word processor. Move the cursor to the space just after *the*, and press the INSERT key. Most word processors then create a *window* at that point on the screen, and you can type in anything you want. When you've finished, press INSERT again, and the window closes around the new material. On a typewriter you would have to type the entire letter again.

We find the ability to insert and delete material electronically does more than speed up the writing process. Because editing and changing material is difficult on a typewriter, our manuscripts gradually turned into a mass of red editing marks. Eventually the draft became unusable, because it was difficult to follow all the changes and corrections. In addition, we often rejected the idea of going through another draft and retyping the document yet another time, because of the time it took. With a word processor, corrections occur as you make them. There is no need to have the document retyped to see how it reads with revisions. If you want to move a paragraph from page 2 to the middle of page 8, most programs let you mark that paragraph and tell the computer to transfer it electronically to a new location. Insertions, deletions, and block moves are accomplished with a few keystrokes, and you see the result of your editing immediately. Some programs even have an *undo* command that lets you go back to the way the document was before the last change, just in case you decide it was better before. We can make our revisions more quickly, and we can do more of them because the boring manual labor has been reduced. Now we can concentrate on the editing process rather than worrying about having the time to retype that report yet another time. What takes only a few minutes on the word processor would take hours with a typewriter.

WHAT MAKES A GOOD WORD PROCESSING COMPUTER?

Large-Capacity Screen Display

The more you can see on the screen at once, the easier it is to compose and edit your document. An excellent word processor has at least a 24-line by 80-character display. In addition, it would be nice to have the ability to display the effect of special printing codes that underline or print words in bold.

The Apple has a 24-by-40 display, but it can be expanded to 80 columns. If you use the 40-column display, you won't be able to see an entire line of text. We recommend that you avoid 40-column word processing. If you are going to use your Apple for professional word processing, you will need the 80-column card.

A Keyboard With Many Function Keys

The more function keys you have, the easier it is to learn and use a word processing program. Most of the special functions can be assigned to a key: just press the key for that operation, and it happens. Without function keys, you may have to remember a complicated routine. On the Eagle PC computer (which we used to write this book), you press the SAVE key, and the computer asks you what you want to name the document. You type in a name and press RETURN. There is less to remember and fewer keystrokes. The Apple IIe keyboard is also a good quality standard typewriter-style keyboard, but it doesn't have programmable function keys.

Fast, High-Capacity, Reliable Mass Storage

Professional word processing calls for reliable, high-capacity disk drives to store documents. Older versions of the Apple II came with a cassette storage system. We would advise against using word processors with cassette systems. You can get the Apple in a one-disk or two-disk version, and up to two additional disk drives can be added. The drives store less than 140K on each disk and are thus considered medium rather than high-capacity drives. They do work reliably and are much less expensive than some of the high-capacity drives used on some other computers.

Plenty of RAM

This may or may not be an issue for you. If you type material no longer than a typical business letter, you will not need lots of memory to hold the document as you type it in. If you type term papers, reports, magazine articles, or books, however, you'll find it very inconvenient to work on a computer with limited RAM. On this point, the Apple IIe gets high marks. The standard Apple IIe has 64K RAM, and 128K is the maximum RAM normally usable on this computer. If you write very long documents, look for a word processing program that lets you use the full 128K. Our first four books were written on a computer with 32K of memory. You can do lots of work with very little memory, but it's not as convenient, and errors are more likely. Our current system has 128K, which will be expanded to 512K soon. An Apple with 64K or 128K can do very adequate word processing, even when long documents are involved.

Freedom from Glitchitis

Glitchitis is a disease commonly found in all sorts of electronic equipment. It generally strikes when a malfunction will do the most damage. It frequently occurs for no known cause and cannot be duplicated when you try to figure out just what happened. Worse yet, it is least likely to happen when you are trying to explain the problem to someone who can fix it. Duplication is possible, however, if you use the computer again for an important task (for instance, for typing the term paper at 1:00 A.M. that is due at 9:00 A.M.). The Apple IIe is remarkably free of the glitchitis disease, although some of its competitors are particularly prone to it.

There are other features to look for when you shop for a professional word processor, but these are some of the most important ones. The Apple IIe has many of the features you need but falls short of perfection in some areas. When you disregard price and compare the Apple IIe to the Eagle PC used to write this book, the Apple IIe comes up lacking. However, in the real world, price must always be considered. The Eagle PC costs $3500, while the Apple IIe with two disk drives costs less than $2000. It is a very cost-effective means of getting good word processing power. A card that lets you use a 24-line by 80-character format is recommended. It costs less than $160.

DESIRABLE WORD PROCESSING FEATURES

Hundreds of word processors are available for small computers. The price range starts at about $60 and goes up to well over $1000. Programs for the Apple IIe are generally priced in the low end of that range, however. A lot of new or revised programs are coming on the market all the time, so by the time you read this, there may be many good programs not even mentioned here. For this reason, we will give you a brief checklist of features to look for in a word processor.

Delete Modes

Ways you can delete text from the screen. Some simple programs permit nothing more than deleting one character at a time. Others have many options. Here are the common ones:

- Delete character.
- Delete word—Deletes material separated by spaces on each end.
- Delete sentence—Deletes material from a capital letter preceded by a space to a period or other end punctuation.
- Delete line—Deletes a line of text on the screen. A poor substitute for delete sentence, since lines on the screen rarely correspond with sentence length.

- Delete partial line—Deletes from cursor to end of line, for example.
- Delete paragraph—Deletes from beginning of indented sentence to beginning of another indented sentence.
- Delete block—See section on blocks for explanation.
- Delete everything—Deletes everything in the memory of the computer.
- Delete undo—Save me from the error of my ways, because I didn't really mean to do that.
- Delete verify—If instructed to delete a lot of material, the program checks (by asking REALLY Y/N? or PRESS RETURN TO DELETE DOCUMENT) before executing the instruction.

Insert Modes

The methods available to add or insert material in an existing document.

- Destructive insert—Replaces material by typing over it.
- Non-destructive insert—Pushes material out of the way as new material is typed in or creates a *window* of blank space where new material can be typed.

Block Modes

A block is a section of text you have marked electronically. You might press the down-arrow key at the beginning of a section and press it again at the end of that section. The computer can then be told to perform different operations on that block of text. Blocks of text can be moved, deleted, or duplicated. Duplicating a block means you can put the same material in several places in the text. Reports often contain many complicated tables that have the same format and different numbers. A complicated table can be typed once, marked as a block of text, and inserted at any point in the text where you want a table. Once you have the table in place, all you have to do is fill in the numbers.

• Delete block—Can a block be deleted?

• Move block—Can a block be moved from one location to another?

• Duplicate block—Can a block be duplicated somewhere else in the document without erasing it from its original location?

• Multiple block—Can more than one block be marked, or is the program limited to one marked block at a time?

Cursor Control

The cursor is a solid or blinking rectangle that tells you where material you type will appear on the screen. It also tells you what will be affected by an instruction to insert or delete material. You must move the cursor over a letter to delete it in most programs. Simple word processing programs let you control cursor movement with arrow keys that point in the direction the cursor will move. On the Apple IIe, most programs use the cursor keys on the bottom right of the keyboard.

• Move by character—The cursor moves one character at a time.

• Move by character, auto repeat—Hold down a key, and the cursor keeps going until you release the key.

• Move by word—The cursor moves to the first letter in the next word.

• Move by sentence—The cursor moves to first letter after an ending punctuation mark.

• Move by paragraph—The cursor moves to beginning of next paragraph.

• End/beginning of line—The cursor moves to end or beginning of line.

• Home—The cursor moves to home position, the top left corner of screen.

• Beginning—The cursor moves to beginning of document.
• End—The cursor moves to end of document.
• Fast scroll—The cursor jumps forward or backward in document several lines at a time.

Search and Replace

If you misspell a word throughout a document, can you tell the computer to find and correct the error? If you have a large document in memory, can you find a particular section by telling the computer to search for a particular word or phrase? There are several variations on the search and replace theme:

• Search for keyword—Looks for a word you specify and moves the cursor to the point where it occurs.
• Replace, once—Finds the target word and replaces it with a new word you specify.
• Selective replace—Finds the target word and asks if you want it changed to the new word specified. You can say yes or no.
• Global replace—Finds multiple occurrences of the target word and changes them to the replacement word you specify.
• Selective global replace—Same as selective replace but checks entire document.
• Wild card search—Lets you specify the target word with *wild card* letters. Telling it to search for Th#mes, for example, means words like Themes and Thames would be found, because the third letter is a wild card, and any letter is acceptable in that position.

Page and Printing Features

• Programmable page parameters—Can the number of lines, the length of line, and the amount of space left at the top and bottom margins be controlled?

• Printer selection—Will the program work with many different types of printers, or is it limited to only one or two?

• Underline—Will it produce underlined text?

• Boldface—Will it produce boldfaced text?

• Large characters—Will it produce expanded or larger-than-normal characters on printers that support that option?

• Italics—Will it produce italicized print on printers that support that option?

• Justification—Will it print justified text, with the right and left hand margins straight?

• Sub/superscripts—Does it support subscripts and superscripts?

• Headers and footers—Will the program let you specify a message that will appear at the top or bottom of each page?

• Page numbering—Will the program automatically number pages for you?

• See/get—Will the program show you on the screen what you will get when the document is printed?

• Wraparound—Will the program automatically move to the next line when you run out of room on the current line? Does it take the word you are typing and move it down to the next line, or does it break the word and leave parts of it on different lines? Breaking words up is a poor substitute for true wraparound that automatically moves the last word typed on a line, the one that is too long to fit, to the beginning of the next line.

This list is not exhaustive. Some of the word processors for the Apple IIe have most of these and many more. However, we feel the list gives you a starting point to evaluate potential programs. You may also want to consider two other types of programs. There are programs that check spelling, although they won't tell you if you used *effective* when you really needed *affective*. Both effective and affective are correctly spelled words and will be accepted by a spelling checker. Words like *affeccived* or *therr* will be caught by the checker. There is also a program called *Grammatik* that looks at the way you use words. It checks for common writing errors and may even make suggestions for improving your writing.

WHAT WORD PROCESSING PROGRAMS ARE AVAILABLE?

There are many different word processing programs available for the Apple. In fact, there are currently at least thirty-five such programs ranging in price from around $50 to more than $500. Space does not permit us to review that many programs, but we will review popular Apple word processors.

You might also be interested in two articles about word processing. *InfoWorld Magazine* published an article entitled *Info-World's Guide to Word-Processing Programs* (Vol. 5, No. 3, p. 27). This article presents information on scores of different word processing programs. Another good article appeared in *Personal Computing* in April of 1983 (p. 110). It's entitled *Word Processing: Finding the Right Software*.

A few paragraphs ago we recommended that you stick to word processing programs that can take advantage of the optional 80-column card for the Apple. Now we're going to break our own rule and begin by reviewing an excellent word processing program that can only display a 38-column line. You'll see why in a few moments.

The Bank Street Writer

The Bank Street Writer has had many Apple owners waxing eloquent with praise since it was introduced a few months ago. It was even given high praise by *The New York Times* and by *Time* magazine.

This new word processing system was developed by Broderbund Software in conjunction with the Bank Street College of Education in New York. It's available for $69.95 from Broderbund.

This word processor was designed to be, above all else, *simple*. And simple it is. The goal was to produce a word processor children can use quickly. It has been estimated that it takes at least ten hours to become comfortable with a word processing system. (We think that's a gross underestimate, by the way.) Educators found that few children were motivated to spend that much time, and many gave up before they could do anything with a word processor. *The Bank Street Writer* is simple and easy to learn.

Even though this program was designed as an educational tool, many adults find it suitable for their needs. If you have never before done a single thing with a computer, this program is for you! If you manage an office where many people are frightened of the idea of word processing, this package is for them!

Now don't get the wrong idea. *The Bank Street Writer* is far from being the ultimate word processing program. But it may very well be the ultimate introduction to computing in general and to word processing in particular.

What makes this word processing program so friendly? First, on one side of the disk there is an excellent tutorial that leads you by the hand as it explains how to use the program. Best

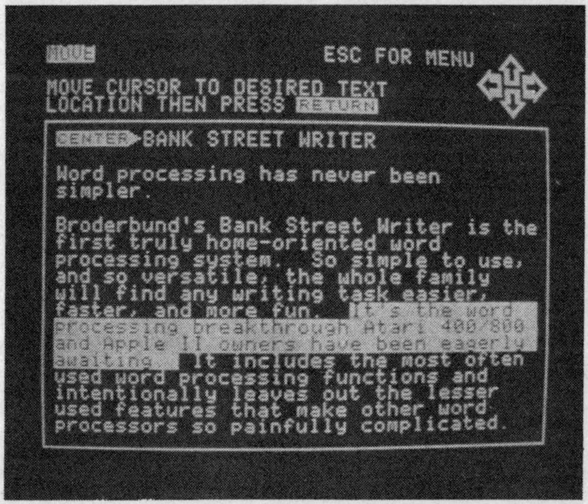

Figure 7.1 Bank Street Writer

of all, it keeps you involved by frequently having you type in text or press different keys.

The tutorial is very well done and ten-year-olds with average reading ability have no difficulty at all with it. For younger children, it's best to have an adult go through the lessons with the child, reading aloud as the tutorial progresses. The lessons are short, and there are frequent opportunities to stop, go over the lesson again, or proceed to the next lesson.

Lesson One teaches you how to enter text, Lesson Two teaches you how to move the cursor, Lesson Three teaches how to use the ERASE and UNERASE commands, Lesson Four teaches the MOVE and MOVEBACK commands, and Lesson Five teaches you to use the FIND and REPLACE commands.

The appeal of this program is ease of use. It isn't a sophisticated, full feature word processor, however. The biggest problem is the short line width. Thirty-eight spaces is simply too short for convenient word processing. But as a learning tool for beginners, or as a word processor for short projects around the house, *Bank Street Writer* is great.

ScreenWriter II

This word processing program finished on top of all others in *Softalk Magazine*'s balloting for the top thirty all-time favorite programs for Apple computers. As a matter of fact, this program finished *fifth* overall, behind three games and *VisiCalc* for the Apple! The program, originally called *SuperScribe II*, is available for $130 from Sierra On-Line.

This program enjoys such wide popularity because it will do so many different things. It will create indices and tables of contents automatically if you flag the words you want. You can *unerase* text you accidentally deleted, you can load and save all or parts of a file, and you can even instruct the program to make footnotes. Then, too, you can display a line up to 70 characters in length.

The way the program handles such a wide display is interesting. It does so without an 80-column board for your computer. In fact, the program can't even make use of the 80-column board, so you can save your money. What *Screen-Writer* does is use the Apple's graphics to create the letters. If you select a ten-character line, each letter will be quite large. If you select a 70-column line, they will be very small. In fact, they will be so small and difficult to read that you definitely need a good quality video monitor. Even that isn't ideal, and you'll find the display difficult to read.

The two main problems with this word processing package are slowness and poor hyphenation. This program is slow in several ways. First, if you type faster than about forty words per minute, you will be going faster than the program, and you will lose some characters. Second, saving, loading, and editing are time-consuming. The hyphenation routine is difficult to learn and doesn't seem to work well.

This is still a good word processing program if you need a variety of features. The program is flexible, and if you don't mind the slow speed, it may be just what you are looking for. The manual is good, and the price isn't excessive. It will display a 70-character line, even if the quality of the display isn't first-rate. If you are looking for a word processor, you should check this one out.

Apple Writer II

This is one of Apple Computer Company's entries in the word processing software field and is available for $150.

One of this program's main strengths is that it will display an 80-character line if you purchase an 80-column board. Be careful about which board you buy. Some, but not all, of the cards will work.

This is a competent word processing program, with good features, like the ability to print form letters. Its deficiencies include the inability to delete blocks of text larger than paragraphs, and a poor manual.

Nevertheless, the program is tried and true, and improvements are sure to come in the future. We know people who have used this program for a long time and swear by it.

Word Handler

Word Handler is a fairly new program available for $199 from Silicon Valley Systems Inc. The company promises free updates as they are released. That's unusual and a real plus!

One of *Word Handler*'s really impressive strengths is the screen display. We mentioned that the best word processors show you on the screen how the printed copy will look. With *Word Handler* you can really do that. You can even see words displayed with centering, boldfaced type, and underlining. That's impressive!

One of the major weaknesses is that you can only print one page at a time without returning to the computer. That might be all right for letters and the like, but a long document would be a real pain to print out using this program.

WordStar

WordStar has been called the Cadillac of word processing programs for the Apple. That's probably accurate. Like all other programs, this one has strengths and weaknesses. We're not going to give this program an extensive review. That's been done over and over again in computer magazines, and we probably couldn't add anything really new. The program is extremely flexible and has many features. That may be one of the problems. Because it's complex, it's not easy to learn to use. It's at its best in an office where it is used often enough for operators to become really familiar with it. This is NOT a program for occasional users. One of its greatest weaknesses is a poorly written and unnecessarily complex manual. Also, it isn't easy to get your hardware set up to run this program. Unless you have extensive word processing needs, you'll probably not want to go with *WordStar*. You don't go rabbit hunting with a cruise missile!

If you use *WordStar* on the Apple IIe, you will need a circuit card with a 280A micro processor on it, and a program called CP/M. *WordStar* will not work on the Apple IIe without them. You thus may end up spending over $300 for accessories and another $300 + for the program.

Spelling Checkers Can Aid Word Processing

Spelling checkers are helpful *add-ons* for your word processor. Spelling checkers look through your document and compare your spelling to thousands of words in the program's dictionary. If you have used a word not listed in the dictionary, the program shows you the word and lets you change it, leave it alone, or enter the word in the dictionary.

Grammar checkers examine your sentence structure and make suggestions for improvements. Some grammar checkers will also look for misplaced parentheses, quotation marks, or other incorrect punctuation, and even alert you to sexist language. Several grammar checkers should be available for Apple IIe computers by the time you read this.

Several companies sell spelling checkers that will work on the Apple. Sensible Software Inc. markets *Sensible Speller* for $125. This fast and easy-to-use spelling checker uses the 80,000-word *Random House Concise Dictionary*. The company has recently produced a new dictionary disk for use with the program. This disk contains 20,000 words from *Black's Law Dictionary*, as well as 15,000 of the most commonly used words from Random House. This should be handy for lawyers. A dictionary disk using *Stedman's Medical Dictionary* is in the works.

DIC-TIO-NARY II is a spelling checker for use with *ScreenWriter II*, *Pie Writer*, and *Apple Writer II*. It has approximately 14,000 words, and you may add up to 1,500 words of your own choosing. The program sells for $99 and is available from Sierra On-Line.

CHAPTER EIGHT

The Apple: Your Business Assistant

If you are thinking about buying a personal computer to help you in business, the Apple is a reasonable choice. It was the first computer to be widely used as a managerial tool. You won't be able to use your Apple to manage the affairs of a firm the size of General Motors, but it can be very helpful in many kinds of business dealings. The Apple IIe is extremely popular as a business tool. There are a lot of reasons for this, but software is the most important. More business software is available for the Apple IIe than for any other computer. There is so much software available that we can give only a brief overview of the business applications of an Apple IIe. For this reason, we won't even describe the small business uses. There are hundreds of programs for the Apple that do general accounting tasks such as accounts receivable, accounts payable, payroll, inventory, and general ledger. Every small business owner is also a manager. Consequently we decided to concentrate on how you can use your Apple IIe as a desktop manager.

Before we start, though, there are several things you should know about the Apple IIe as a business or managerial computer. First, you'll need some extra equipment. Managerial programs tend to be memory-hungry, and they generally run on computers with disk drives. You will therefore want to buy at least the single-disk-drive version of the Apple IIe with 64K of memory. We recommend the two-disk-drive version with 128K of memory, and some applications may require more floppy disk drives or a hard disk drive. Many managerial applications will require a modem, and a printer is usually essential.

You may also want to investigate the use of CP/M on the Apple IIe. CP/M is a popular operating system used on business computers. Thousands of business and managerial programs are available for computers that use CP/M. You will need to buy a CP/M card and an 80-column card for your Apple, but they are worth the price. Not all CP/M programs will run on your Apple, but many of the CP/M programs for business applications are available in Apple-compatible formats. Between those and business programs that run under the regular Apple operating system, you can find almost anything you want for the Apple IIe.

THE APPLE IIe AS A MANAGER'S COMPUTER

If you are a manager, you know the importance of information. If you can control and manage information better, you're likely to be a better manager. There are many different ways you can use your Apple IIe to help you manage your business. We expect that telecommunications will be an extremely important managerial tool in the future. It is already helping managers communicate better and faster. If you plan to use your computer for telecommunications, we strongly suggest that you read Chapter Six. Pay particular attention to the comments about The Source. The Source has an option called *Management Contents* that's well worth the price of admission. *Management Contents* helps you research most of the popular business magazines and can even give you short abstracts of articles. In one session using *Management Contents*, you may be able to save enough time to pay for both your Apple IIe and The Source subscription. Better yet, you will probably find things that you would have missed using any other method.

Spreadsheets

The most useful managerial tool for people in business is probably the spreadsheet. Accountants and others who perform financial analyses have been using spreadsheets for a long time. A spreadsheet is simply a rectangular worksheet containing rows and columns of numbers. This type of form is used because it makes it easier to keep the numbers organized in relation to all others on the form. The most basic example of a spreadsheet is a column of numbers with a total.

Now what happens when one of the numbers in the column is changed? The total for that column is wrong! If you are doing your work by hand, and you change several numbers in several columns, you will have to recalculate the totals. The larger the number of rows and columns on the work sheet, the more complicated it becomes to change any one number. Imagine how many hours of work would be involved in changing and updating a complicated financial forecast.

You can avoid much of this tedium by using your Apple IIe and an electronic spreadsheet, which does the same thing the hand-made spreadsheet does, with the computer doing much of the tedious and repetitive work. A variety of electronic spreadsheets are available for the Apple IIe computer and almost every other small computer.

VisiCalc

VisiCalc was the first electronic spreadsheet program for personal computers. So many people use *VisiCalc* that it is the most popular software product in history! *VisiCalc* has been so successful many other companies have written similar, sometimes better programs. Today there are more than sixty different electronic spreadsheets available for small computers!

VisiCalc has been such a success because it cuts down on the amount of work you must do when you use a spreadsheet.

In fact, if you have *VisiCalc*, most of what you have to do is to get the numbers and information into the computer. After that, simple commands tell the computer to rearrange the information in almost any way you want. With *VisiCalc* you can:

- Get the total of the values of any series of locations. For example, all of the top row or all of the first column.
- Get the average for any series of numbers.
- Try different values on your data to get projections.
- See certain data organized in a graph, which can be sent out to your printer.

For example, assume you are a district sales manager for a large company. You have been asked to prepare a sales estimate for the next fiscal year that gives three different levels of performance. You supervise twenty-five sales representaties, your company has 350 products that range in price from $3.95 to $225, and you have nineteen different discount plans. Your regional manager wants your sales estimate by next week, and you just found out about it today. You have two choices: get an Apple IIe and *VisiCalc* or get a different job! Believe it or not, you could probably do the complicated sales analysis described in just a single afternoon with *VisiCalc*.

How does *VisiCalc* do all this? Your computer screen becomes a window showing you a certain section of a giant spreadsheet made up of 254 rows and 64 columns. This window is easily moved around with the direction keys on the computer. You can look at any portion of the spreadsheet you want. The screen can even be split into two different parts. This is an excellent feature to use when you need to make comparisons. It is also handy when you have forgotten what data were entered in a different part of the worksheet. You can also ask the computer to search for certain kinds of information, do some calculations, and show you the result. You can also find out what is in any given portion of the worksheet at any time.

Once you have entered a formula, you never have to enter it again. You can copy formulas, headings (or titles), and numbers into as many columns as you want. Using our sales estimate as an example, suppose you want to show what would happen if ten of the sales reps had a twenty-five percent increase and all the others had a five percent decrease. All you have to do is tell the computer to multiply your first results by either twenty-five percent or minus five percent wherever appropriate. The computer performs all of the calculations.

Don't get us wrong, though. A program that will do as much for you as *VisiCalc* will take time to learn. But if you have to do any kind of financial projections, your time and effort will be very well spent. Even though you can get started quickly, you will have much to learn, and it will take some practice before you can take full advantage of all of the things *VisiCalc* can do.

VisiCalc was developed by VisiCorp and lists for $250. It is available in most computer stores or directly from VisiCorp.

Training Aids for VisiCalc

When you buy *VisiCalc*, you get a user's manual. But like any manual, it will be more useful to some people than to others. Because *VisiCalc* is designed to do so much, you may need some tutoring that goes beyond the manual. A number of companies have developed training materials for this purpose.

Cdex Training for VisiCalc is a computer-assisted training program. This is an excellent, user-friendly way to learn about *VisiCalc*. The program is $49.95 and is available from Cdex Corporation.

VisiCalc Worksheets from Padware Limited is another product designed to help you use *VisiCalc* more effectively. A package of fifty sheets of paper designed to help you plan how you will use *VisiCalc* sells for $10.95. There are two excellent books on *VisiCalc* that can replace the user's manual. *The VisiCalc Book Apple Edition* by Donald Bell (Reston Publishing) is an excellent tutorial that will help you learn the ins and outs of *VisiCalc*. Barbara Chirlian's *Simply VisiCalc* (dilithium Press) will introduce you to *VisiCalc*. It is a good book to read before you decide to buy the program.

Programs to Supplement VisiCalc

There are a great many programs intended to add capabilities to *VisiCalc*. There is no way we can tell you about all these supplemental programs, but we can give you a thumbnail sketch of a representative few. You must have *VisiCalc* to use these programs.

Viz-A-Con is a disk program intended to supplement *VisiCalc*. It sells for $139.95 from Abacus Associates and is designed primarily to make it easier to consolidate data. With it you can *roll up* days into weeks, weeks into months, departments into divisions, divisions into companies, or do any other consolidation of *VisiCalc* data.

VisiTrend/Plot is a handy program (also from VisiCorp) for calculating business statistics and for printing graphs and charts from data generated by *VisiCalc*. It sells for $300 and works with Epson MX-80 and MX-100 printers and a few others. You will probably not be ready for this complex program until you are very familiar with *VisiCalc*.

Solutions, Inc., produces three software packages designed to let you do some special things with *VisiCalc*. They are *VIS\Bridge/REPORT*, *VIS\Bridge/SORT*, and *VIS\Bridge/DJ*.

VIS\Bridge/REPORT is a report writer you use to tailor your printouts. In other words, you don't have to be bound by the page length and width restrictions of *VisiCalc*. You can rearrange the material you have in your *VisiCalc* file and print it out in a report format that suits your needs at the time. This package sells for $79.

VIS\Bridge/SORT is a different way of sorting material in your files. You can sort the rows or columns of your spreadsheet into either ascending or descending sequences. You can sort either alphabetic or numeric items. You can use five columns or rows as sort keys. Partial spreadsheets may be sorted while headings and totals remain in place. The price of this software is $89.

VIS\Bridge/DJ is the most unusual of the three packages. You can use it to receive up-to-date financial information from the Dow Jones News/Retrieval Service and load it directly into *VisiCalc*. You can update your business forecasts based on the latest stock market information. This program sells for $259.

32 VisiCalc Worksheets is a program from dilithium Software. Many of the things you will want to do with *VisiCalc* have already been done. These adaptable worksheets are designed to do a variety of things, such as job estimation, net worth, energy use, micro-economic analysis of inflation, and tenant records in apartments. The package is available as a book (you type in the material you want to use) for $19.95, or a book and diskette set for $34.95.

Database Management

A database management program will help you keep track of the mountains of information needed to conduct business. Database management programs are electronic filing systems. Why do you need an electronic filing system? One reason is that there's probably a lot of wasteful duplication in current files. A personnel department, for example, probably has quite a bit of information on each employee. They have to keep track of data such as names, addresses, next of kin, and so on. The sales department probably also maintains a file on each salesperson. These files contain some unique information but probably also contain much of the same information that is in the personnel file. Within departments, it's the same story. Duplication is wasteful of time and space, and that translates to dollars and cents.

If you are currently doing some of your business information housekeeping with computers, you probably still have the same problem. You may be using a payroll program, and you may be using another program to keep track of the amount and type of each sale made by each salesperson in your department. The ideal way to handle this information is to have one central electronic file, which is accessed by all other programs. That eliminates duplication and saves money. It also means that you can centralize your *data gathering* efforts. Since there is only one file, you can be very thorough and do a really good job.

When information needs to be updated, it only has to be entered once.

dBase II

dBase II is one of the best of the database management systems for the Apple IIe. There's good news and bad news about this software. The good news is that the program is very flexible and can do a super job for you if you use it correctly. The bad news is that the program is expensive ($700) and difficult to learn to use effectively.

dBase II is what is referred to as a *relational database* system. What that means, in a nutshell, is that the program is constructed in such a way that it is easy to pull out and understand the *relationships* existing among the information bits stored in the system. For example, suppose you decide you want to know the relationship among total sales in February, numbers of sales staff on the road in that month and the previous month, and the amount of money spent on advertising over the past six months. Using separate paper and pencil files, that information could be hard to get. With *dBase II* it would be at your fingertips.

Reviewers of this program have said it has *almost unlimited flexibility*. You'll have to pay a price, of course. And the seven hundred dollars may be only the beginning. The real price is in terms of complexity. This program is not for beginners! Learning to use *dBase II* has been compared to learning to speak a new language! You don't just slip the disk in and go with *dBase II*. If you have no computing experience, this probably isn't for you. But if you have a business operation with information problems, and if you or someone in your organization has had some experience with computers, *dBase II* may be just what the doctor ordered.

One piece of good news is that you can give the program a try without risking $700. When the program arrives, it comes with a sample disk to allow you to try out the program. If you aren't happy, don't unpack the real program. Just send it back for a full refund. That's a nice touch. You'll need extra memory and at least one disk drive to run this program.

There is now a very good book on the market to help beginners get started with *dBase II*. It's called *Everyman's Database Primer*, by Robert A. Byers, and it's available from Ashton-Tate, the same company that markets *dBase II*.

Instant Recall

Instant Recall is a database management program for people who aren't ready for *dBase II*. Available for $59.95 from Howard Sams & Co., this program is much simpler and easier to use than *dBase II*, but it won't do as much. Essentially, it is an electronic card file. You can't use it to sort entries either alphabetically or numerically, but it will search for any word, number, or record number in any file. Although it is not sophisticated, this is a good way to learn about database management programs.

Other Business Software for Your Apple

There are a lot of other business uses for the Apple IIe computer that we haven't talked about. A few will be introduced here.

TeloFacts

TeloFacts is a new kind of program available from dilithium Software. This software is *documentation-based* rather than *program-based*. The documentation for *TeloFacts* is a book, *How To Use TeloFacts*, which is available separately for $9.95. The program helps you design, administer, and analyze questionnaries. The book not only teaches you how to use the program, it also teaches you how to design questionnaires.

The program can be used for any questionnaire that has multiple-choice answers. For instance, a personnel manager could use it to evaluate job applicants. A bank loan officer could use it to evaluate loans, and a teacher could use it for testing. *TeloFacts* is most often used for marketing surveys. It will rank, score, and evaluate the answers to any given set of questions. *TeloFacts 1* sells for $49.95 and is available in many bookstores. *TeloFacts 2* is a more sophisticated version of the program that sells for $195. The strongest feature of this program is that it is extremely easy to use.

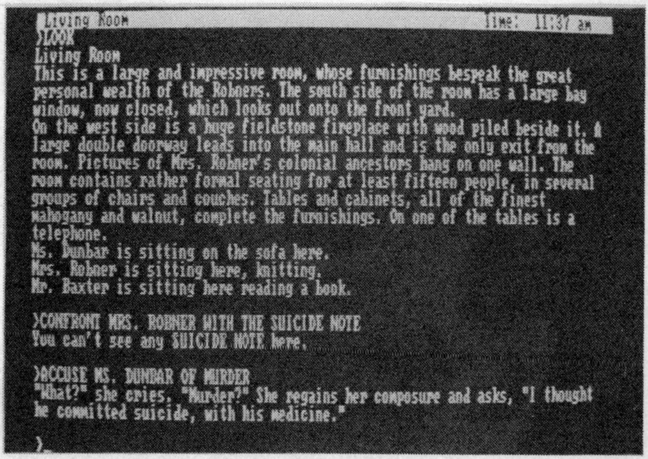

Figure 8.1 TeloFacts

Dow Jones Market Analyzer

The *Dow Jones Market Analyzer* is available for $350 from Dow Jones and Company. You will need to have access to the Dow Jones database, *Dow Jones News/Retrieval Service*, to be able to use this program. It is similar to the information utilities described in Chapter Six.

Investors refer to this program as a tool for *technical analysis*. That's investor jargon for looking at how a stock has done in the past and using this information to project future performance. The program is easy to use, and a sample lesson comes with the package.

CHAPTER NINE

Programming

THE APPLE IIe'S PROGRAMMING LANGUAGES

The Apple in your home or business understands several computer languages. No, it doesn't converse fluently in French or Spanish, but it does understand a language called BASIC, as well as PILOT, FORTRAN, and Pascal. The concept of a *computer language* is difficult for new computer owners. What is a computer language, and what role does it play in the computer?

The first thing you should know is that computer languages serve much the same purpose as human languages. They are a means of communication. Consider the way two people communicate. For the moment, assume you are a cooking instructor. Today you are going to teach a student how to cook a souffle. Because you and the student both speak English, you can give your instructions in English. This means English is your language or medium of communication. The information you communicate to the student in English is a specific, step-by-step set of instructions. *Recipe* is the special term used to describe such a set of directions when you are cooking.

If your student speaks French, and you speak only English, you may have a very strange looking souffle! To get what you want, there must be a common language between the two of you. The same thing can happen with a computer. Computers like the Apple IIe speak their own set of languages. Computers cannot learn English, so you will need to learn one of the languages the computer understands. When you learn a computer language like BASIC, you can communicate with the computer much as a master cook communicates with a student. Instead of communicating recipes, you will give the computer *programs*. A computer program is an organized set of instructions that tell the computer how to accomplish a particular goal. All the programs reviewed in this book are really instructions someone has written to tell the computer how to do a job. Programs, like recipes, are created by humans.

Learning to program a computer is not something everyone should do. Learning how to use the computer to do a job or play a game is just as honorable a goal as becoming an experienced computer programmer. Learn to program the computer only if you find programming interesting.

LEVELS OF COMPUTER LANGUAGE

Suppose you are thinking of learning a second human language. If your first language is English, there are some languages, like French and Spanish, that are similar to your native language. Others, like Greek and Latin, are not as similar, but contain some familiar elements. Still other languages, like Japanese and Chinese, are so different that few elements will be familiar to you. To learn Chinese you need to learn a completely new alphabet that bears no resemblance to the one you learned as a child. In addition, the way information is organized is quite different.

If you decide to learn a computer language you will find the analogy relates. Some, like BASIC, are not exactly English, but there are enough similarities so you don't feel completely abandoned by your native tongue. Others, like FORTRAN or Pascal, are not so much like English, but they still contain some familiar phrases or terms. Still others, like 6502 machine or assembly language bear little resemblance, if any, to English. We would advise you to learn one of the more English-like languages before tackling an assembly or machine language.

Computer languages have two basic parts: the vocabulary and the rules for using the vocabulary. These rules are usually referred to as the grammar. The word PRINT, for example, is a part of the vocabulary used in the Apple IIe's BASIC. When the computer finds this word in a program, it looks for material to display on the screen. A rather extensive set of rules tells you how to organize and punctuate the material after PRINT. These instructions tell the computer exactly how you want your material displayed on the screen. However, it is relatively easy to remember that PRINT is one of the words in the vocabulary of BASIC and to remember that PRINT tells the computer what to do. Things are not so easy with some languages.

High-Level Languages

BASIC is only one of several languages that make up the category of *high-level languages*. High-level computer languages like BASIC use English-like words and work with decimal numbers (the type we learned to add, subtract, multiply, and divide in grade school). While the other two families of languages, machine and assembly languages, are written specifically for a particular *computer*, high-level languages are often developed for a particular *purpose*. One of the older computer languages, FORTRAN (FORmula TRANslator), is the language most used by universities and scientists. COBOL (COmmon Business Oriented Language) is a popular business language, and BASIC (Beginners All-purpose Symbolic Instruction Code) is the best known of the easy-to-learn general purpose computer languages. Every popular personal computer sold today understands at least one, if not several, dialects of BASIC.

Programming Languages for the Apple IIe

There are several different programming languages available for the Apple IIe computer. The issue of special equipment like cards and boards becomes very complicated with the Apple IIe computer. There are so many alternatives that you can easily be misled. When you shop for programming software, be sure to find out if you need to buy additional software or hardware to use the product you are buying.

We'll discuss some advantages and disadvantages of each language, show you a simple example of what some of the languages look like, and describe some of the things you can do with each. And we'll tell you what kind of equipment you'll need.

BASIC for the Apple II Computer

The obvious place to begin is with the language that is most commonly used. BASIC is ready for you to use when you turn on the Apple IIe computer. BASIC is a high-level language. It is also a general purpose language. It can be used for almost any type of programming and is many times easier to learn and to use than-low level languages like machine or assembly language. BASIC uses English and English-like words instead of cryptic number or letter codes. For example, if you want the computer to put a certain word on the computer screen, you can just tell it to "PRINT" that word. Or if you want the computer to add 3 and 2, and assign the sum to X, you can tell it to "LET X = 3 + 2."

If dealing with so many different computer languages is not confusing enough, there is one more complication. Not only are there over 150 different languages, there are also many different versions, or dialects, of each language. Just as there are many different dialects of French and English, there are also many different dialects of BASIC. The reason is complicated, but in part it comes back to the idea that we need different tools to do different jobs. You probably always use a hammer to pound a nail, but you may use a different type of hammer to pound different types of nails.

One reason there are many different dialects of BASIC is that different computer manufacturers keep refining the language so that it will keep pace with the new hardware they develop. As with other computers, the BASIC used with the Apple IIe computer has gone through a number of refinements. The latest version is called Applesoft BASIC, which is built into the hardware of the Apple IIe computer. As soon as you start up the Apple IIe, Applesoft BASIC is there, waiting to be used. If you have an Apple II+ or an Apple II, you have a dialect of Applesoft BASIC that is slightly different from the Applesoft BASIC for the Apple IIe. The changes are only slight and were made to enhance the special hardware features of the Apple IIe.

There are other dialects of BASIC available for the Apple IIe computer. Integer BASIC, for example, comes as part of the standard disk operating system for the Apple IIe series. When you equip the Apple IIe with a disk drive system, you use a *D*isk *O*perating *S*ystem called DOS 3.3. When you power up the disk drive system, you have a choice of using the built-in Applesoft BASIC or Integer BASIC. Integer BASIC is stored on the same disk as DOS 3.3. Integer BASIC has some advantages of its own. It has a built-in program that checks for errors as you type in each BASIC instruction. There are also some things that Applesoft BASIC can do that Integer BASIC cannot. For example, Integer BASIC is unable to deal with decimal numbers, where as Applesoft BASIC can. Applesoft BASIC is a good high-powered version of BASIC and will do all you need for most general purpose programming jobs. Integer BASIC is less powerful but may be a little easier to use.

Other dialects of BASIC sold mainly by third-party software companies can run on the Apple IIe. Some versions are faster than Applesoft or Integer BASIC.

Some BASIC language programs are called *compiler programs;* they translate the instructions of a program written in BASIC back into machine language all at one time. The program, now in machine language, is then stored, and when you run the program, it runs very fast. Applesoft and Integer BASIC on the other hand, are *interpreter programs*. They translate BASIC instructions to machine language as the program is running. The program is always stored in BASIC. Language programs that use interpreters are easier to work with than those that use compilers, but the interpreter programs are slower. A variety of BASIC language programs use compilers instead of interpreters. At most Apple dealers, you can buy a BASIC compiler called *Applesoft BASIC Compiler*. This product is sold by Microsoft Consumer Products for $175. A compiler that has lots of good features and has gained popularity among many Apple IIe programmers is called *The Einstein Compiler*. This compiler BASIC program is sold by The Einstein Corporation for $119.95. It is hard to find fault with *The Einstein Compiler*. There are other third-party compilers available that are good, and if you already have one, you probably wouldn't want to switch, but if you are just thinking about getting into compiler BASIC, this is a good place to start.

Pascal

Pascal is a sophisticated high-level general purpose language. Apple does not sell a Pascal language program, but several are available. If you are interested in programming in Pascal, *Pascal/M* is available from Digital Marketing for $395. This version of Pascal will satisfy most of your needs and is easy to use. However, if you want to use a more advanced version of Pascal, you can get *UCSD p-System Pascal* from PCD Systems. The UCSD part of the name means that it is a dialect of Pascal developed at the University of California at San Diego. This version of Pascal is very powerful and is used by many different personal computers. It costs $650, but if you want to use Pascal for serious programming, it might be worth the price.

PILOT

PILOT is short for Programming Inquiry Learning Or Teaching. This is another specialized high-level language and, as the name suggests, it was designed to be used in education. Apple has two versions of PILOT called *PILOT* and *Super PILOT*. Both require disk drives. *PILOT* sells for $100 and *Super PILOT* is $200. PILOT is quite different on different computers. Each computer company that developed PILOT for their computer designed it to fit some of the specific characteristics of that computer. The Apple version of PILOT uses the color graphics and sound capabilities of the Apple computer.

Logo

Logo is a specialized high-level language. This language was especially designed to help children learn and to help them learn about computers. It is interesting and easy-to-use. Apple has been one of the leaders in developing and refining this language. You'll find a more detailed discussion of Logo in Chapter Four.

Assembly Language

About the closest most computer programmers come to programming the actual internal workings of the computer is *assembly language*. Because programming in machine language was so hard, early computer workers developed this language. Assembly languages use letters of the alphabet as codes for instructions. The advantage of this to the programmer is that the program is much easier to understand, and the codes are much easier to remember and use. For example, the code for telling the computer to add the number 2 to the number 3 would look like this in one machine language:

11 001110 00000011 11001110 00000010

While in an assembly language part of the program could look like this:

AC I 3
AC I 2

Although ACI 3 probably doesn't mean anything to you, to the person who knows assembly language it means: "Add the number 3 to the number in the accumulator," a special memory location in the CPU. And likewise, ACI 2 means "now add the number 2 to the accumulator." ACI 3 would be much more likely to remind you that 3 was being sent to the number accumulator than 11001110 00000011, wouldn't it? The point is that very few people have to program in machine language today. Usually the lowest-level language used is assembly language, and assembly language is available for your computer if you want to use it.

Your Apple IIe computer is not ready to be programmed in assembly language when you turn it on. You will need to buy a software package. Software packages for programming the Apple IIe in assembly language are usually called *editor/assembler* packages. The software also contains a program that will change your instructions written in assembly language to machine language so that the computer can act on them. Often these editor/assembler packages have other special programs as well, most commonly short programs written in assembly language and ready to include in other programs. These short programs are called *subroutines*. They do many of the common things most programmers want. For instance, almost all packages have a program that will alphabetize a set of words. If an alphabetizing subroutine were included in an editor/assembler package, you could simply add it whenever you wanted to use it in your program, and you wouldn't have to write those subroutines yourself.

As with everything else relating to the Apple IIe computer, there are several different editor/assembler packages available. One of the most popular is *Apple Tool Kit*, sold by Apple for $75. This package has enjoyed a good reputation among Apple IIe programmers and includes all of the features you will generally need in an assembly language package. Another editor/assembler is *EDIT 6502*. This package is sold by LJK Enterprises for $99.95 and is more suited for the beginning assembly language programmer than the *Tool Kit* version.

We should caution you, however, that assembly language programming is not a good place to start. It is so difficult that there is a high risk you'll become discouraged before you ever get your computer to do much. Most editor/assembler instruction manuals state that you should not try to use the program unless you have already had some experience with assembly language. There is clearly a much easier place to begin programming.

EXAMPLES OF APPLE IIe PROGRAMMING LANGUAGES

To give you just an idea of what the different languages look like, we will show you how a very simple computer program is written in different languages. Keep in mind that there are many different dialects of each language, and the programs you see in this chapter are only intended to show you what a language looks like. You may not be able to type the program into your computer and get it to run. If you want to get started programming, you will need an instruction manual for the version of the language you are using. A good book on that language written for beginners is also recommended.

Each of the sample programs we show you will instruct the computer to do the following:

The computer puts on the screen

HI, I AM THE APPLE IIe COMPUTER

WHAT IS YOUR NAME?

You type your name, let's say Bob. The computer puts on the screen

NICE TO MEET YOU, BOB

High-Level General Purpose programming: BASIC and Pascal

Applesoft BASIC belongs to the family of the most popular programming language today. Two aspects of BASIC have made it so popular. First, it is a general purpose language that can be used quite efficiently for almost any programming job. Second, it is very easy to learn. If you have never learned a programming language and want to get started programming your Apple IIe computer yourself, BASIC is a good place to start. The advantages of BASIC as your first language are:

- Every other brand of home computer can be programmed in BASIC. Even though the dialects are slightly different, you can easily adjust your programming skills to another computer.
- Since more programs are written in BASIC than any other language, you can adopt and adapt more programs for your own use than you could if the only language you knew were one other than BASIC.
- Since it is the easiest general purpose language to learn, you can probably do more in BASIC with less learning time and effort than with any other language.

Here's what our computer program looks like in Applesoft BASIC:

```
10 HOME
20 PRINT "HI, I'M THE APPLE IIe COMPUTER"
30 PRINT "WHAT IS YOUR NAME";
40 INPUT N$
50 PRINT "NICE TO MEET YOU,"; N$
60 END
```

Pascal, while it is much easier to use than assembly language, is more complicated than other high-level languages such as BASIC. Pascal has three main advantages:

- It is faster than other high-level languages, meaning that a program written in Pascal will run faster than the same program written in another high-level language.
- Because of the way Pascal is structured, a program written in this language is very easy for another Pascal programmer to understand and to modify.
- Because of its speed and power, Pascal is a more efficient language for some complex business and scientific uses.

Our program written in UCSD Pascal looks like this:

```
BEGIN
WRITE(OUTPUT, 'HI, I AM THE APPLE IIe');
WRITE(OUTPUT, 'COMPUTER.');
```

```
WRITE(OUTPUT, 'WHAT IS YOUR NAME?');
READLN(INPUT,NAME);
WRITE(OUTPUT, 'NICE TO MEET YOU,');
WRITE(OUTPUT, 'NAME);
END
```

Specialized Programming for Teaching and Learning

Although enthusiasts of this group of languages claim that they are really suited for many general purpose programming tasks, they are becoming popular primarily because they are highly suited for classroom use. In addition, they are very easy to learn. Logo is becoming extremely popular. Chapter Four talks about Logo as an educational tool, so we need not say much more about it here. Remember that this language is so easy to get started that very young children can program in Logo after only a few minutes of instruction. If you have children who now use or will use your Apple IIe computer, Logo would be a good investment. Our program looks like this in Logo:

```
TO GREET
CLEARSCREEN
PRINT (HI, I AM THE APPLE IIe)
PRINT (HOME COMPUTER)
PRINT (WHAT IS YOUR NAME?)
CALL READLINE "N
PRINT "HELLO,
PRINT :N
END
```

PILOT was created for a very specific purpose: to let teachers write programs that help teach children. These programs are called *computer-assisted instruction*. Many teachers do not have the kind of technical background required to quickly learn and use complex programming languages. Yet teachers are in a better position than anyone else to know what kinds of programs are most needed in their classrooms. PILOT is a language teachers can learn quickly. It is designed to do the kind of programming required to get the computer to act as a teaching machine. PILOT is sometimes called a conversational language. With only a few programming skills, a teacher can write a program that makes the computer seem almost human in the way it responds to answers the students type in. It seems to understand what they say and can talk to them.

PILOT is *not* the best general purpose language around. But, if you are a teacher, and you want to do some programming that will give your children some drill and practice activity, you may want to get started with PILOT. PILOT is also one of the quickest ways to get children started programming. In PILOT, our program might look like this:

```
D: R$(15)
T: HI, I AM THE APPLE IIe
T: COMPUTER
T: WHAT IS YOUR NAME?
A: R$
T: HI THERE $R$
E:
```

Low-Level Programming

Using an editor/assembler package, you can program your computer in assembly language. Remember that in this language you are only one step removed from the language the computer really understands, machine language. When you tell the computer to carry out the instructions you have given it in assembly language, a built-in program called an assembler translates your instructions into machine language, and the computer carries them out.

Although programming in assembly language is quite complicated and tedious, there are some good reasons to learn it. Probably the greatest advantage is speed. Although the Apple can do things very fast compared to how fast you and I can do them, sometimes a little additional speed is needed. Programs written in assembly language can do things much faster than programs written in high-level languages like BASIC.

A second advantage to using an assembly language is you can get the computer to do some things you can't get it to do in other languages. In this language you have total control over the computer. The only limits to what you can do are limits set by the engineering of the computer. In high-level languages, you are confined not only by the engineering limits of the machine, but by the limits of the language. Because assembly language gives you total control over the computer, you can use the language in two different ways. First, when you need a program that would be impossible or very awkward to write in a high-level language, you can write the program in assembly language using an editor/assembler package. Second, rather than writing a whole program in assembly language, you can write a short program that does one special thing and then incorporate it into a BASIC or other high-level language program.

Now let's see what the program might look like if you were to write it using an editor/assembler package:

```
         REF    WMBW,INPUT
LINE1    TEXT   "HI, I AM THE APPLE IIe"
LINE2    TEXT   "COMPUTER"
LINE3    TEXT   "WHAT IS YOUR NAME?"
BUFFER   BSS    32
LINE4    TEXT   "NICE TO MEET YOU,"
GREET    LI     R0,0
         LI     R1,LINE1
         LI     R2,32
         BLWP   @VMBW
         LI     R0,64
         LI     R1,LINE2
         BLWP   @VMBW
         LI     R0,128
         LI     R1,LINE3
         BLWP   @VMBW
         LI     R0,BUFFER
         BLWP   @INPUT
         LI     R0,256
         LI     R1,LINE4
```

```
BLWP    @VMBW
LI      RØ,288
LI      R1,BUFFER
BLWP    @VMBW
END     GREET
```

Even More Languages

There are many other languages available for the Apple IIe that we haven't mentioned. Two of these are popular on large computers but not very widely used with personal computers. Both FORTRAN and COBOL can be used with the Apple IIe. These languages have been in use for a long time and have some special applications. If you have just purchased an Apple IIe computer or are thinking about purchasing one, you will probably want to start with BASIC. If, however, you have used one of these languages on a large computer and feel comfortable with it, you will be glad to know that you can talk to your new friend, the Apple IIe, in a familiar language.

FORTRAN

FORTRAN is a popular language with people who work with mathematical formulas. In fact the name FORTRAN comes from the words FORmula TRANslation. The Apple version of FORTRAN, *Apple FORTRAN*, costs $200. Another version of FORTRAN available from Microsoft, is a compiler instead of an interpreter. It sells for $195.

COBOL

COBOL, like FORTRAN, is a popular language with large computers. As the name suggests, it is a specialized language for business. COBOL uses many regular English words. Although its use with personal computers is limited, it can be run on many brands and is available for the Apple IIe. A version of COBOL that is compiled rather than interpreted is sold through most Apple dealerships for $750.

Some Special Tools for Programming

Computer languages, like computers, can be thought of as tools. The question of which tools you need and which are best can only be answered when you know what job you want to do. As you have seen, the Apple IIe computer has a good variety of languages available for it. Whether just for fun or for work, hopefully both, you should be able to do as much of your own programming as you like. There are many other programming tools in addition to the language programs themselves. They are designed either to give you short-cuts in programming or to speed up the running of your program once you have written it.

Advanced Operating Systems sells a product called *The PROGRAMMER*. This program will help you organize and design a program written in BASIC. You can take some short-cuts in the actual programming process: you will be able to use one instruction to accomplish what would otherwise take a series of instructions. This program, however, is most useful to the professional programmer. Programs like *The PROGRAMMER* are difficult to understand if you are not already experienced in BASIC or some other language. However, if you are an experienced programmer and are looking for some specialized tools to add to your programming tool kit, *The PROGRAMMER* could be of value to you. It sells for $199.95.

A Word of Advice

As you have learned from reading this chapter, there are many different languages available for the Apple IIe. You will probably be very content with Applesoft BASIC. It is built right into the computer and needs no extra software or hardware. At some time though, you may want to expand your programming tool kit to include some other dialects of BASIC or some other languages. The decision of which dialect of which language to use is always complicated, but is even more complicated with the Apple IIe. The complication comes with the fact that there are so many alternatives. We suggest that before you consider using any language other than Applesoft BASIC, you talk to an Apple dealer or a representative of the company that sells the product. Make sure you clearly understand what you will need to use that language on your computer. It is very easy to get caught in the trap of always needing just one more piece of hardware or software to be able to use the language of your choice.

CHAPTER TEN

Peripherals

This chapter could have been called *Ways to Spend Your Money*. Peripherals are the extra pieces of hardware you buy for your computer to get it to do different jobs. Remember when you last looked at new cars? The first price quoted you was just for the bare-bones car. Then you added up all the things that went along with it. Each item made the car a little nicer and each one had a price tag.

Computer parts can be put roughly into seven groups:

- Input devices
- Central processing unit or CPU
- Memory
- Output devices
- Devices for both input and output
- Mass storage devices
- Interfaces

Some computers are built with almost everything you need in one case. Other brands include only the bare essentials. You have to start adding on as soon as you walk out the door of the computer store. The Apple IIe is designed to fit somewhere between these two extremes. With the Apple you get most of the essential parts of a computer built into one case. You also get a computer that is designed to let you add parts quickly and easily. The main advantage of this type of system is that it gives you lots of flexibility. You might think of it as a smorgasbord where you can build your own dinner, as opposed to ordering from the menu where what you see is what you get.

When you buy the Apple IIe computer, you get a central processing unit, some memory, a keyboard for getting information into the computer, and a speaker for sound effects. With just this bare-bones computer you won't be able to do much. Getting the rest of the parts and getting them connected is very easy, however. There are two other essential devices: a video display and some type of mass storage device. You can use an ordinary TV set for your video screen, and you can use a cassette tape recorder or disk drive for mass storage.

A vast array of peripherals is available for the Apple IIe computer. Some of these peripherals are almost essential if you are going to do very much computing with the Apple IIe. Others are very nice features that you can use to do more and do it more easily. Other peripherals are for very highly specialized uses. Not only are there many types of peripherals, but there is an almost unbelievable number of different brands, makes, and models of each type. We will tell you about the different types of peripherals and give some specific examples.

INPUT DEVICES

Before you can do much with a computer, you have to be able to get information into it.

The Keyboard

The keyboard is, of course, the most familiar input device. For many purposes it is also the most efficient device. When you are doing word processing or just giving the computer messages, the keyboard is an efficient input device. For other

Figure 10.1 The Apple IIe personal computer

purposes, such as drawing pictures on the computer screen, the keyboard becomes tedious to use.

Other input devices have special features that make them good for doing certain jobs. One of the main jobs that requires a different input device is graphics, which is just another word for pictures. With the Apple IIe, you can do some graphics by just using the standard keyboard on the computer. But some things that can be done with graphics are awkward with the keyboard. As a result, computer companies have developed a variety of peripherals that make graphics work quicker, easier, and better.

Joysticks and Paddles

A joystick is the little gadget with the handle sticking up that you use to play video games. They sometimes have buttons that can be used to fire rockets or do other things. A paddle is similar to a joystick except that, instead of a long handle, it has a short knob. For all practical purposes, joysticks and paddles do the same thing. Basically, their function is to move the cursor around on the screen. You move the joystick handle to the right, and the cursor moves to the right on the computer screen. You move the handle forward, and the cursor moves up the screen.

Both joysticks and paddles come in lots of sizes, colors, and shapes. They vary widely in price and in the special features they offer. Good quality joysticks can be bought from HW Electronics for $39.95 each. If you want a top-of-the-line joystick, you can buy the *Super Joystick* from Peripherals Plus for $59.95. Apple sells its own brand of paddle for $39.95, or you can buy a more sturdy version from Computer Works for $49.95.

Beginning in August 1982, *Creative Computing* magazine ran a three-part series on joysticks and paddles. These articles will tell you everything you ever wanted to know and more.

Light Pens

A light pen is a pen-like pointer connected to the computer. By touching the light pen to the computer screen, you can give the computer information. One common use is to indicate your choice on a multiple-choice test or questionnaire. Or you could use it to move the cursor around on the screen. If you were using a light pen in this way, you could get the impression that you were actually drawing on the screen with a stream of light. This, of course, is not really what is happening, but the result is the same.

To get the light pen to do these things, you have to have a program that tells the computer how. The *LPS II Light Pen System* is one possibility, if you are interested in using a light pen with your Apple IIe. This system gives you a high-resolution light pen system with full software support. Pictures, diagrams, and other graphics can be drawn directly on the screen. This system sells for $349 and is sold by Gibson Laboratories.

A Trackball

This device is a ball mounted in a case. You roll the ball in one of four directions. The computer is able to count the number of times the ball turns. As you move the ball, the cursor moves on the screen. You can draw pictures on the screen by just moving the ball around on a large surface. The trackball, like all other input devices, has to have the right software before it can do its thing.

The Mouse

This mouse is a computer mouse. It is a palm-sized device with a small trackball on the bottom. When you move the mouse, the cursor moves around on the computer screen in relation to where the mouse is on your desk top. In other words, the top of your desk is like a giant computer screen. If you move the mouse to the bottom left corner of your desk, the cursor moves to the bottom left corner of the computer screen. The mouse has some obvious uses for computer graphics. You can use your desk top as a large drawing pad. As you move the mouse, the computer draws a picture on the screen. The mouse is one of the quickest and easiest devices for moving the cursor on the screen and it can be used on a variety of surfaces.

Mouse devices are becoming quite popular; at least a dozen are available for the Apple IIe. One of the leading mouse makers is Mouse House. Their mouse sells for about $300.

One use being made of both the mouse and the trackball is as a remote control for a lecturer. If you are giving a talk and are using a computer to help you present your visual displays, you can use one of these devices to control a cursor-like pointer on the screen. As you stand at the front of the room or walk around the room you can move the trackball or the mouse around on a small rectangular board and thus move the pointer on the screen.

Voice Input

This type of input is developing rapidly and is now available for the Apple IIe computer. It has an air of science fiction about it. You can speak to the computer in your native tongue, and the computer will follow your instructions. There is still a way to go before this type of device is perfected, but it could become an important peripheral device for computers like the Apple IIe in the near future. High quality voice input systems are still a few years away, but there are some devices that will obey simple commands. For instance, if the computer has a program telling it to ring the dinner bell, you can just say, "Ring the dinner bell." A good example of this kind of system is called *WALDO* from Artra, Inc. As you might have guessed, this type of system is expensive. The complete *WALDO* system will cost about $800.

Excalibur Technologies Corporation is working on a system called *Savvy*, which will be able to accept normal speech patterns as instructions for the computer. It can learn new words as you go along, so if you don't always say things the same way, it will still understand you. *Savvy* is a complete programming package. You can use it to write your own programs, even if you don't know how to program. It sells for about $900.

MEMORY

Memory can be thought of as storage space where the computer can store information and retrieve it whenever it wants. The size of memory space (or how much information the space will hold) is measured in kilobytes. A byte is enough memory to store one character. A byte is made up of eight smaller pieces of information called bits. Memory space is referred to in terms of kilobytes or K. K stands for 1024. If someone tells you that their computer has 16K of memory it means that the computer will store 16,384 bytes of information (16 × 1024). Some computers will hold so much memory that it is measured in millions of bytes. Just over one million bytes of memory (1000 × 1024) is called a megabyte.

One problem with most home computers is that when you buy the basic model, you don't get very much internal memory. So you are limited in the software you can use and the length of programs you can write. The least amount of memory you can get with the Apple IIe is 64K. You can expand the memory to 128K, or you can buy the computer fully loaded with 128K to start with. Much of the new software designed for the Apple IIe requires more than 64K.

Solid State Disk Emulators

This type of peripheral is an external memory device that lets the computer send a batch of information out to external memory so that it can go out and get it at any time. One such device, called the *Interstellar Drive*, will store about one megabyte of information that can be called up by the computer when you tell it to do so. This peripheral is sold by PION, Inc., for $1095. Solid state disk emulators do the same job as regular disk drives but work much faster. You must still save the data on a regular disk drive before switching off the computer.

Buffers and Spoolers

For all practical purposes, buffers and spoolers do the same thing. They send some information out to a temporary storage device, where it will be passed on to another peripheral such as a printer. Their main function is simply to free the computer up so that you can keep on working while your printer is printing. Without a spooler or buffer, you may find yourself waiting for your printer to print out a document and wishing that you could get back to your writing. With a spooler, you can send the document out to it in a few seconds and get back to typing. In the meantime, the spooler feeds the document to the printer as fast as it can print it.

MicroSpooler is a high quality spooler available from Consolink Corp. for $199. There are many buffers available for the Apple IIe. They range in price from $100 to $300, depending on the amount of information they will hold and their quality.

OUTPUT DEVICES

Monitors

The most common output device, of course, is a video screen. You have two choices on this item. You can either use your TV set, or you can buy a specially built monitor. Apple sells a small device called a *Color TV RF Modulator* that you use to connect a color TV set to your computer. Generally speaking, a monitor, since it is designed for this purpose, gives you the best quality. There is a wide variety of monitors to choose from, and since this is one part of the computer that is relatively problem-free, you can shop around for the best price without much worry of ending up with a bad purchase.

You can use a black and white monitor or television with the Apple, but by doing so you are losing one of the very best features of the Apple computer, the color graphics. A good choice in color monitors, if you want to shop around, is the *Amdek Color I Monitor*. This monitor sells for between $375 and $400. Many other good color monitors are available, however.

Printers

One of the first things many computer owners like to add to their basic computer system is a printer. Why do you need a printer?

• Program listings and data reports are easier to read on paper than on the computer screen.

• When you have your program printed on paper (hard copy), you have protected yourself against losing it if you have equipment failure or a power outage.

• With a printer and the right software, you can use your computer as a word processor (see Chapter Seven).

If we reviewed all of the printers available for the Apple IIe computer, we could end up with a whole book, and by the time we were done, it would need a complete revision because new printer models come out every week. We will tell you some of the things you need to be aware of when shopping for a printer, and then we'll describe some representative types.

There are four things you should look for in a printer:

- Quality of print.
- Speed of print.
- Cost.
- Special capabilities such as graphics and plotting.

When selecting a printer, you are always dealing with trade-offs. If you choose a very cheap printer, you might get low quality print, slow speed, and no special features. If you choose a very high quality at a relatively low cost, you will get slow speed. If you get more speed at a relatively low cost, you will get lower quality. If you want both speed and high quality print, you may pay as much for your printer as you did for the rest of your computer system.

The printer situation today is far from gloomy, however. Things are getting better all the time. Many low cost printers with very good quality, fair speed, and some special features are available. We will tell you about three different types of printers and review some that work well with the Apple IIe.

Thermal Printers

A thermal printer uses special chemically treated paper and puts images on the paper with a heat process. The major ad-

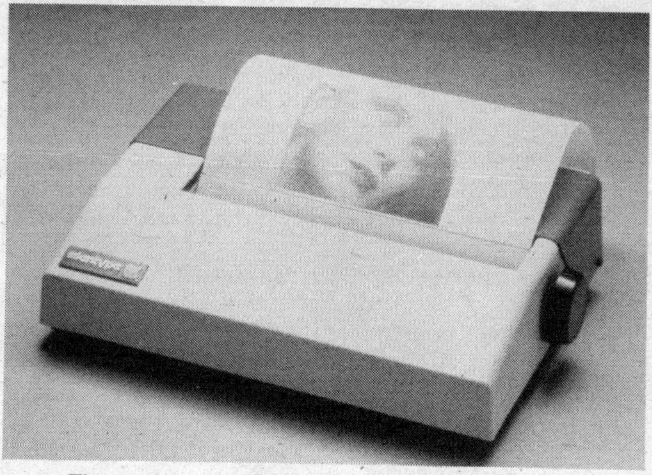

Figure 10.2 The Apple Silentype Thermal Printer

vantage of these printers is quiet operation. Some of the latest models can print extremely quickly and provide a wide variety of print styles. A major disadvantage is the cost of the special paper. When other types of printers use just plain paper, it is hard to justify buying expensive treated paper.

Apple sells a quiet, versatile, and compact thermal printer called the *The Apple Silentype Thermal Printer*. The price on this printer is $350.

Impact Printers

Thermal printers are not nearly as popular with personal computer owners as impact printers are. An impact printer uses a system in which a metal or plastic object strikes against a ribbon that is pushed against the paper, leaving an imprint on the paper. There are two main types of impact printers: *dot matrix* and *daisy wheel*.

Dot Matrix Printers. These printers produce the type of print we all recognize as being printed by a computer. Each letter is formed by a series of dots. The quality of the print varies but is getting better all the time. Some of the newest versions have such a tight pattern of dots that the letters look almost as if they were printed with a typewriter. Since these printers are impact printers, they do not require special paper. Dot matrix printers are cheap and quite fast. But since the print does not look like typewriter print, they are not considered *letter quality* printers. The print quality is getting so good now, however, that some people are beginning to use them for ordinary office work.

If you use a printer for printing out computer programs and doing graphics, a dot matrix printer will work well for you. However, if your primary need is for word processing, you may want to look at another type.

Dot matrix printers can be selected from a staggering array of prices, qualities, and brands. Almost any computer store you enter will have several models ranging in price from a low of $199 to a high of $2500. They vary as much in speed and quality of print as they do in price. Our suggestion is that you visit several local computer stores and ask for a demonstration of printers that work with the Apple IIe.

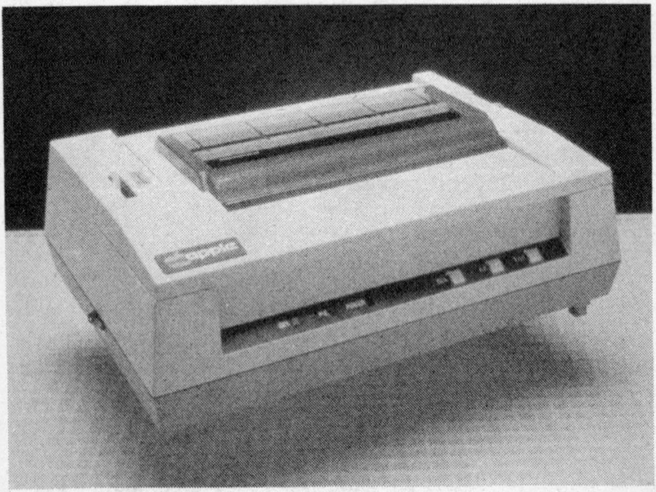

Figure 10.3 The Apple dot matrix printer

A very popular dot matrix printer is the $700 Epson FX-80 printer. This printer will print about three pages per minute and has some very good special features including graphics. It weighs only 12 pounds and is both durable and reliable.

Daisy Wheel Printers. This type of printer will print fully formed letters and characters as clear and crisp as those made by a typewriter. This means the printed letters are made up of solid images rather than dots. The daisy wheel printer gets its name from its print element, which looks like a daisy with long petals coming out from a central wheel. There is a letter, number, or character at the end of each prong. The daisy wheel spins around at a very high speed. When the correct letter is properly positioned a small hammer strikes it against a ribbon, which makes an imprint on the paper. These printers also use plain paper.

Until recently, these printers were very expensive. However, they have begun to drop in price and are becoming competitive with the dot matrix printers. The main difference between the two types of printers is speed. The low-cost daisy wheel printer is much slower.

One of the most popular low-cost daisy wheel printers available for the Apple IIe is the Smith-Corona TP-1. This printer retails for about $600, is easy to use, seems to be very reliable, and gives a high quality print. The great disadvantage to this printer, as you might have guessed, is its speed. It takes just a little over two minutes to print one full page. Nevertheless, this is a good printer for the home computer owner who wants letter quality and doesn't need a lot of speed.

Some Other Considerations

Three other pieces of information are important for using a printer with the Apple IIe:

- Nearly every printer comes in two different types called *serial* and *parallel*. Serial printers accept data a bit at a time, and each character code is made up of seven or eight bits. Parallel printers accept data eight bits at a time over eight separate data lines. As a general rule, the parallel type is the easiest to use.

• When you buy a printer, we highly recommend that you look carefully at buying a tractor feed to add to it. With a tractor feed, you can use continuous feed paper. The sheets are all hooked together and just keep on going through the printer. Without a tractor feed, after about six to eight sheets of continuous paper have gone through the printer, the paper will often slip sideways.

• If you use a serial printer, you will need to have an RS-232 interface. This device is described later in this chapter. Parallel printers require a parallel interface.

Speech Synthesizers

When a computer is equipped with a speech synthesizer, it can convert printed words into spoken words. Keep in mind that this means words spoken by the computer, which has a strange accent. The quality of speech is getting better but still sounds like something from a science fiction robot.

There are many uses for speech synthesis:

• As a prompt for education and computer-aided instruction programs. With a voice synthesizer, the screen is free to display graphics and other detailed data rather than just directions and prompts.

• As an aid to verbally and visually handicapped people. Both outgoing and incoming messages can be transmitted easily and with a surprising degree of understanding.

• As an aid to using business programs. A bookkeeper can input names and account balance and hear confirmations and totals without looking at the screen.

• To make personal programs more lively and entertaining. The personalized flavor helps attract and hold attention.

To get your Apple IIe computer to talk to you, the first thing you need is a speech synthesizer. There are at least a dozen models available for the Apple IIe. Intex Micro Systems

Corporation sells a good quality speech synthesizer called the *Intex-Talker* for $295. A speech synthesizer that is much cheaper, called *The Echo*, is sold by Street Electronics Corporation for $145.95.

MASS STORAGE

One of the most urgent needs of any personal computer user is to have a method of storing large amounts of information outside the computer. When the computer is turned off, the information in its memory is lost if it hasn't been stored someplace else. It is not very practical to spend hours writing a program or doing word processing and then have to start all over the next morning after you turned off your computer. The family of peripherals that handle this problem is called mass storage systems.

Cassette Recorders

The first personal computers used cassette recorders for mass storage. The cassette recorder is still quite popular, even though many computer owners are now going to other systems. The cassette recorder has three serious limitations as a mass storage device:

• It is slow. Compared to the speed at which you can type in information, the cassette recorder is fast. Compared to disk storage systems, it is very slow. It works fine for some uses, but after waiting five to ten minutes for a program to load or save onto cassette tape, you will start wishing you had a better system.

• It does not have random access. When you have more than one program on a tape, and you want the computer to find and load a certain program, you either have to find the right place on the tape yourself or start the tape at the beginning and let it run until the right program comes along.

• Poor reliability. Some dedicated tape users will argue differently, but cassette tape is notoriously unreliable as a storage system. If the slowness of the cassette system doesn't make you covet a disk system, the first time you lose three hours' worth of work when you thought you had it all stored on tape will.

Despite the disadvantages of the cassette tape system, there is one major advantage. It is called PRICE! A variety of recorders will work, and most can be bought for less than $80.

Disk Drive Systems

A floppy disk is small, usually 5½ inch, disk that looks sort of like a phonograph record. It is very thin and can bend

Figure 10.4 Floppy disk

Figure 10.5 Disk II: single disk drive

easily—thus the name floppy. When they are inserted into a disk drive the computer can store information magnetically on them. The biggest advantage of the disk system is that it saves information from the computer and loads it back into the computer many times faster than a cassette. Programs can be found quickly by the computer, it doesn't have to spend a lot of time searching, as it does with cassette. The disk system is also many times more reliable than the cassette system.

We suggest you get a least one disk drive with your Apple IIe. Although one drive is far better than no drives at all, a second drive allows you to do some things you just can't do with one drive. If you buy the bare-bones computer and decide to add two disk drives later, it will cost you $545 for one drive and $395 for a second drive. Each drive actually sells for $395, but you can't use a drive without a disk controller card that sells for $545 with one drive. These prices are all for Apple's disk drives. Many other companies sell drives and controller cards for the Apple at much lower prices.

Hard Disk Drives

A higher capacity, faster mass storage system is the hard disk drive or, as it is often called, the Winchester drive. These are the most technically advanced mass storage peripherals available for small computers. They are sealed units in which the magnetic surface is protected from contact with an injurious environment. Particles of dust, tobacco smoke, or a spilled cup of coffee cannot reach the stored information. The amount of information that can be stored on a hard disk ranges from five to twenty million characters. The reliability of these units is greater than that of a floppy disk. There are also some disadvantages to these systems, the main one being price. They are at least five times as expensive as a floppy system.

For those who really need or just want the best, a variety of hard drive systems are available for the Apple IIe. Apparat, Inc., sells their *Hard Disk Subsystem* for $1,995. Apple's hard disk system for the Apple IIe costs much more.

INTERFACES

Some peripherals are mentioned only in relationship to other peripherals. They are called interfaces. They actually do a variety of things and some have some built-in programming, but their main function is to act as a go-between for other peripherals and the computer. Sometimes they act like small computers themselves. They take information from one source, modify it in some way, and pass it on to another source. Their job is one of keeping all the different parts of a computer system talking to each other. The main thing we need to mention here is that when you buy any peripheral you need to check closely to see which, if any, of these interfaces you need.

One of the very good features of the Apple IIe computer is that interfaces and sometimes complete peripheral systems can be added very easily. Most of the interfaces you will need for the Apple IIe come in the form of cards that plug into the expansion slots inside.

These interface cards, like all aspects of the Apple IIe computer, come in an astonishing range of shapes, sizes, and types. They will do many different things, and new ones are being marketed every day. The type of interfaces you need will depend primarily on the peripherals you add to your computer.

One interface that becomes almost a must for most Apple IIe owners is the RS-232 card. This interface can be bought in a variety of different ways, depending on whether you buy just the plain RS-232 card or buy it in conjunction with something else. Just this card alone will cost about $100. Many printers require a parallel interface card that costs around $80.

SPIKE PROTECTORS

One type of peripheral that really doesn't belong in any of the groups we have talked about in this chapter, is called the *spike protector*. This is a simple device that plugs into a wall socket. You can then plug your computer and its peripherals into the spike protector. The purpose is to protect your computer from high voltage spikes or glitches in the electrical power supply. This is important because dirty power can cause permanent damage to your computer and its peripherals.

A good source of spike protectors is Kalglo Electronics Co., Inc. which has a whole range of spike protectors. Spike protectors are available for prices that range from $20 to $800, with most priced between $35 and $150.

One last note on peripherals: whenever you connect a piece of equipment to your computer, you will need some type of connecting cable. These can often be quite expensive, so make sure they are either included in the cost of the peripheral, or you find out the price before you buy the peripheral.Otherwise you may find yourself with a new device that you can't use because you can't connect it to your computer.

* * *

We have tried to give you an idea of the vast array of different items that can be added to the Apple IIe computer. We have not even covered all of the different types of peripherals available, much less all of the different makes and models. When you set out to add peripherals to your Apple IIe computer, we suggest you do some careful shopping at your local computer stores and read recent issues of one or two computer magazines that publish articles of interest to Apple owners.

This concludes *Things to Do with Your Apple IIe Computer*. We hope that you have enjoyed it and have learned some useful things. If you haven't bought a computer yet, you might want to read some of the other books in the series. Buying a computer can be either an enjoyable or frustrating experience. How much you enjoy your computer may depend on how much you find out about it before you buy it.

Glossary

Address: Main memory in a computer is like a grid of thousands of individual boxes. Each memory location (or box) is called an address.

Alphanumeric: Information presented in both alphabetic and numeric form, for instance, a mailing list. The numbers 0–9 and the letters A–Z, or any combination.

Applesoft BASIC: This is the standard BASIC available on Apple computers. Applesoft BASIC is ready to use when you turn your computer on.

Apple Writer: A word processing program for the Apple.

Applications software: Programs designed to perform specific tasks. Applications software can be games, educational programs, or business programs.

Arithmetic expression: A group of letters, numbers, and/or symbols that tell the computer to perform an arithmetic function. For example:

2+2
2*2
A22
2/4
2/A
A*(2/B8)

Arithmetic operator: A symbol that tells the computer to perform an arithmetic operation. The operators include + addition; − subtraction; * multiplication; / division; and ∧ raise to a power.

ASCII: A simple code system that converts symbols and numbers into numbers the computer can understand. For instance, when you type *a* on the keyboard of your computer, the binary number 01100001 is sent to computer's central processing unit (CPU). The CPU then displays the letter *a* on the screen.

Assembly language: A low-level programming language that is much faster than a high-level language such as BASIC. Assembly language programs are extremely difficult to write. Here are two lines from an assembly language program:

```
LDA
MOV C,A
```

BASIC: Beginner's All-purpose Symbolic Instruction Code. A high-level computer language designed for beginners. Apple IIe BASIC is a dialect of BASIC designed especially for the Apple II microcomputers. Here are three lines of a program written in BASIC:

```
10 PRINT "HELLO HOW ARE YOU?"
20 INPUT A$
30 GOSUB 500
```

Baud: A unit of information transfer. In microcomputers, a baud is one bit per second.

Baud rate: The rate at which information is transferred. For instance, 300 baud is a transfer rate of 300 bits per second. The Apple IIe is an eight-bit computer. This means that each character, space or symbol requires eight bits. Therefore, a baud rate of 300 transfers only 37.5 characters per second. If you are sending a letter with each word approximately six characters long, and you have one space between words, you can send about five words a second or 300 words a minute.

Binary number: A number system that uses only two digits, 0 and 1, to express all numeric values. See digital computer.

Bit: The basic unit of computer memory. It is short for binary digit and can have a value of either 1 or 0.

Black box: A piece of equipment that is viewed only in terms of its input and output.

Boot: The process of loading part or all of the disk operating system into the computer. This lets you load information from the disk or save information to the disk.

Buffer: A temporary storage place used to hold data for further processing.

Bug: A problem that causes the computer to perform incorrectly or not at all.

Bus: A set of connection lines between various components of the computer.

Byte: A group of eight bits usually treated as a unit. It takes one byte to store a unit of information. For instance the word *love* requires four bytes.

CAI: Computer-Aided Instruction.

Canned software: One or more programs that are ready to run as is. The game *Deadline* is canned software.

Cartridge: A 2 × 3 × ¾-inch plastic box that contains ROM software such as BASIC. The Apple does not use cartridge software.

Cassette: A small plastic cartridge that has magnetic tape inside. The tape is wound from one reel onto another. Computer programs can be stored on a standard audio cassette.

Cassette drive: A standard tape recorder used to save (record) or load (retrieve) computer information.

Cathode ray tube (CRT): The picture tube of a television set or monitor. It is used to display computer output.

Central processing unit (CPU): This is the heart of the computer. It contains the circuits that control the execution of instructions.

Chip: A formed flake of silicon or other semiconductor material containing an integrated circuit.

Circuit: The complete path of an electric current. A computer circuit may have thousands of different elements, for example, transistors, diodes, and resistors.

Circuit board: A plastic board that has hundreds or even thousands of different circuits.

Clock: An electronic circuit in a computer that is the source of timing and synchronizing signals.

Code: A system of symbols and rules for representing, transmitting, and storing information.

Coding: Designing a computer program.

Command: An instruction that tells the computer to perform an operation immediately. The command RUN, for instance, tells the computer to begin immediately executing a program.

Compiler: A computer program that translates high-level language statements into machine language.

Computer-Aided Instruction: The process of teaching by computer. This is a system of individualized instruction that uses a computer program as the learning medium.

Console: The keyboard and other devices that make up the control unit of a computer.

Control key: Pushing the computer's control key in conjunction with another key causes the computer to perform special functions. For instance, the Control key pressed in conjunction with *C* interrupts Apple programs.

Controller: A device that can be attached directly to the computer or to an external mechanical device so that images on the screen can be moved around. A joystick is a controller.

CP/M: A special operating system that runs on many different computers.

CPU: Central processing unit.

CRT: Cathode ray tube.

Cursor: The little flashing square on the CRT that indicates where the next character will be displayed.

Daisy wheel printer: A printing machine whose print head has a number (usually 96) of radial arms or petals. Each petal has a type character on the end. Daisy wheel type is equal to or better than most typewriter type.

Data: All items of information a computer can process or generate—numbers, letters, symbols, facts, statements, and so on.

Database: The entire collection of data in a computer system that can be accessed at one time.

Database management system: A program that organizes data in a computer's data storage so that several, or all, programs can have access to virtually any item, and yet a particular item need be keyed into the computer system only once.

Data processing: The process of converting data into machine-readable form so the computer can work on it.

Data transmission rate: Baud rate.

Debug: To eliminate errors in a computer program or a computer.

Decimal number system: This is the number system you are familiar with, that is 0–9.

Default: See default value.

Default value: An assigned quantity for a device or program that is set by the manufacturer. For instance, a printer may have a default value that tells it to print everything in elite type. A default value in a program is usually the most common or safest answer. As another example, a word processing program may ask if you want to clear everything in memory. The safest answer is no, since it doesn't cause any harm if you hit the wrong key. In this example the program would have a default value of no.

Desktop computer: A complete computer system designed to fit on a desktop. The Apple is a desktop computer.

Device: Any piece of computer equipment.

Digital: A system that uses the numbers 0 and 1 to represent variables involved in calculation. This means that information can be represented by a series of offs (0) or ons (1). See bit.

Digital computer: A computer that uses a series of electronic offs and ons to represent information. These offs and ons are converted to (or from) binary numbers. The Apple is a digital computer.

Directory: A list of all the files on a diskette.

Disc: Disk.

Disk: A flat circular piece of mylar that is coated with magnetic material. It is used to store computer information. See also hard disk and diskette.

Disk drive: An electromechanical device that stores on or recalls information from a disk. Up to four disk drives can be connected to the Apple IIe.

Diskette: A flexible disk that is 5¼ inch in diameter (about the size of a 45 RPM record). It is the most common mass storage device. The Apple uses diskettes as the primary means for mass storage. However, you can also use cassette storage. See floppy disk.

Disk file: An organized collection of data stored on a disk.

Disk operating system: An operating system that lets the computer use one or more disk drives. See operating system. The Apple computers run Apple DOS, but you can buy a special card that lets the computer run CP/M.

Documentation: All of the available information about a particular computer, computer program, or set of programs, such as how to turn on the computer, how to load programs, and so on. For computer programs, the documentation should include such information as what type of computer the program runs on, how much memory is needed, and how to operate the program. The Apple IIe comes with an owner's manual. Other manuals tell how to use an 80-column screen card, disk drives, Apple DOS, and so on.

DOS: Disk operating system.

Dot matrix printer: A printer that forms characters as patterns of dots. The dots lie within a grid of definite dimensions, such as 5×7 dots.

Dual density: A technique of writing twice as much information on a diskette.

Edit: To make changes on the screen in data or a program.

Electronic mail: Personal or other messages generated on computer and transmitted to another computer at a different location. The computers are connected by phone lines.

Escape: To interrupt execution of a program. The Apple has a control key labeled ESC. When you press the ESC key, the program quits running. The computer tells you what line number it was on when program was interrupted.

Execute: To operate a computer program or part of a computer program. The process a computer goes through when it analyzes instructions and acts on them.

Expansion slot: A special connector on the inside of the Apple. It is used to add peripheral devices. If you take the top off an Apple computer and look inside, you will see seven black slots that are one half inch high and three inches long. These are the expansion slots.

Expression: A combination of numbers, variables, and operators that can be evaluated. The answer must be a single number or variable. For instance, 2+3=5. It can't equal 7. Other expressions such as A+B, A−3 or A/B*38 must also have only one answer.

External memory: Mass storage.

Field: A unit of information that is part of a file. For instance, in the following mailing list file, NAME, ADDRESS, CITY, STATE and ZIP are all fields:

Sample Mailing List
NAME________________
ADDRESS________________
CITY________________
STATE________
ZIP________

In this example, both the information and title are part of a field. For instance, the field for Joe Jones is this: NAME Joe Jones.

File: An organized collection of related records. A payroll file has a complete payroll record for each employee.

Floppy disk: Diskette.

Formatting: The process of electronically organizing a diskette so that information can be stored on it and retrieved from it.

FORTRAN: FORmula TRANslation. A high-level computer language used for mathematical or engineering applications. Here are three lines from a FORTRAN program:

```
40 FORMAT (E14.7)
   X=A+B*C/D-E
   WRITE (6, 50)X
```

Graphics: Pictures, line drawings, special characters, and so on that can be displayed on the screen or produced by a printer. The Apple IIe can produce sophisticated graphics.

Hard copy: A copy of the computer's output printed on paper.

Hard disk: A rotating mass storage device that uses a rigid disk made of a hard plastic-like material. It has many times the storage capacity of a diskette.

Hardware: The various physical components of a computer system, for instance, the computer itself, the printer, keyboard, and monitor.

High-level language: A computer language that uses simple English words to represent computer commands. For instance, the command PRINT "Hello" in BASIC tells the computer to print the word *Hello* on the screen.

Initialize: To set a program element or hardware device to an initial quantity (usually zero).

Input: To transfer data from the keyboard or a mass storage device into the computer's internal memory.

Input device: A device used to enter information into a computer. These are all input devices: keyboard, joystick, disk drive, cassette player.

Input/Output: The process of entering data into a computer or taking it out.

Integrated circuit: A group of components that form a complete miniaturized electronic circuit. The circuit has a number of transistors plus associated circuits. These components are fabricated together on a single piece of semiconductor material.

Interactive: A computer system that responds immediately to user input.

Interface: A device that allows other devices to communicate with each other. A modem, for instance.

Inverse video: A process that shows dark text on a light background on your screen. Normally light text is shown on a dark background.

I/O: Input/output.

Jack: A plug socket on a computer.

Joystick controller: A two-inch by two-inch black box with a movable plastic stick on the top of it. It is used as an input device most often with computer games.

K: When used as a measure of computer memory, K is an abbreviation for kilobyte or kilobytes. It is also an abbreviation for kilo.

Kilo: A prefix meaning 1000. In computer jargon it is used as an abbreviation for 1024.

Kilobyte: 1024 bytes. Thus 4 kilobytes (abbreviated 4K) of memory is about 4000 bytes of memory. It is exactly 4096 bytes, but 4K is a convenient way to keep track of it. This means that if you have 4K of memory, you have space for 4096 characters, spaces, numbers, and symbols in your computer.

Language: A means of communicating. The difference between computer language and human language is that a computer language allows humans to communicate with computers. The lowest level of language is machine language, the *pure* language of the computer. Machine language programs use 1s and 0s to represent the offs and ons in the computer. Machine language programs are the most difficult programs to write, but they do not have the speed and action limitations of high-level languages. Assembly language programs are also low-level languages, but they use simple mnemonic statements as commands. High-level languages, like BASIC, FORTRAN and Logo, use English-like statements to tell the computer what to do. BASIC is the most common language, because it is the simplest to use.

Line number: A number that defines each line of programming in a high-level language. Each line of the program begins with a line number. The computer executes the program in line-number order, starting with the lowest number.

Load: The process of entering data or programs from an external device, such as a disk drive, into the computer. If you load a program into the computer, it is available for use.

Logic: A systematized interconnection of devices in a computer circuit that cause it to perform certain functions.

Logical operator: A symbol that tells the computer to make a comparison. These operators include > (greater than), < (less than), and = (equals).

Logo: A high-level computer language that is often used by children. An easy-to-learn language, Logo allows colorful, detailed graphics to be drawn on the screen. Sprite graphics and turtle graphics are terms associated with Logo. A version called *Apple II Logo* is sold by Apple Computer.

Loop: A series of programming instructions that repeat. The last instruction in the loop tells the computer to return to the first instruction. Intentional loops have some means of escape built into them. Unintentional loops, caused by programmer error, can only be stopped by pressing the escape key or turning the computer off.

Low-level language: A computer language at the machine level (a pattern of pure binary coding). It is neither simple nor obvious for a human being to read, understand, or use.

Machine language: The lowest level language. It is a pattern of ones and zeros that the computer understands.

Mail merging: A program usually used with word processing that allows you to insert names and addresses into a group of documents. All you have to do is load the names and a sample of the document; everything else is automatic. For instance, suppose you want to send the same letter to 2000 people. Once you have created the mailing list and the letter, the computer adds the name and address of the first person to an original copy of the letter. It can also address the person by name at several different places in the letter. It does the same thing for the second person on the list, the third, and so on.

Mainframe computer: A large, expensive computer generally used for data processing in large corporations and government installations. Originally, the term referred to the extensive array of large rack and panel cabinets that held thousands of vacuum tubes in the early computers.

Mass storage: The files of computer data that are stored on media other that the computer's memory. For example, diskettes and cassettes are mass storage devices.

Matrix printer: Dot matrix printer.

Mega: A prefix meaning one million.

Memory: The internal hardware in the computer that stores information for further use. The Apple IIe has 64K of memory.

Menu: A display shown on the screen that gives you a list of options. You select an option by typing a letter or number and pressing the return key.

Microcomputer: A fully operational computer that uses a microprocessor as its CPU. Microcomputers are a new kind of computer. Whereas minicomputers are small scale versions of large computers, microcomputers are an outgrowth of semiconductor technology. Consequently, some microcomputers have features not found on either minicomputers or mainframe computers.

Microprocessor: A central processing unit contained on a single chip.

Minidisk: Diskette.

Minicomputer: A small computer based on large computer technology.

Mnemonic: A technique or symbol designed to aid the human memory. Its most common computer use is in assembly language programming. For instance, it is much easier to remember LDA (an assembly language term) than 004000 072.

Mnemonic code: A system of abbreviations designed to replace obscure, complex terms used in preparing assembly language programs.

Modeling: A partial simulation of real or possible situations.

Modem: A modulating and demodulating device that enables computers to communicate over telephone lines.

Monitor: A television or cathode ray tube used to display computer information. In common usage, a monitor usually refers to a special device used exclusively for computer output.

Mylar: A type of plastic used in the manufacture of floppy disks.

Nano: One billionth.

Nanosecond: One billionth of a second. Modern computers operate in nanoseconds.

Numeric data: Data that consists entirely of numbers.

Operating system: A set of computer programs devoted to the operation of the computer itself. The operating system must be present in the computer before applications programs can be loaded or run.

OS: Operating system.

Output: Information or data transferred from the internal memory of the computer to some external device.

Output device: A device used to take information out of a computer. CRTs, mass storage devices (such as disk drives), and printers are all output devices.

Packaged software: Canned software.

Parallel: The performance of two or more operations or functions simultaneously. For instance, a parallel port accepts all eight bits of a byte at one time. Some computers are connected to the computer by the parallel port.

Pascal: A powerful high-level computer language for business and general use. Named for French mathematician and philosopher Blaise Pascal (1623–1662). Here are three lines from a Pascal program:

```
BEGIN
READLN (I,HOURS)
IF I=1 THEN WORK:=SUN
```

PC: Personal computer.

Peripheral: Any device that connects to a computer. Printers, joysticks, and modems are peripherals.

Personal computer: Microcomputer.

PILOT: This is an easy-to-learn, high-level language designed for use by novice computer users. Primarily used for educational programs.

Pixel: A picture element that is one point on a screen. The size of the pixel depends on the computer graphics mode being used and the resolution capabilities of the screen.

Port: The location where input/output devices are connected to the computer. For example, a printer may be connected to computer with a cable at the parallel port. A modem may be connected at the serial port.

Powerful: As used with computers, powerful means that a computer, a device, or a program has a lot of features. Powerful is so *over used* in the computer industry that it really has no meaning.

Power supply: A device, consisting of a transformer and other components, that converts household current (115 or 230 volt) to the voltage used by a computer.

Printer: A device for producing paper copies (hard copy) of the data produced by a computer.

Program: An organized group of instructions that tells the computer what to do. The program must be in a language the computer understands.

Prompt: A symbol, usually a question mark, appearing on the screen that asks you to enter information.

QWERTY: An abbreviation used to indicate a standard typewriter-style keyboard. The first six letters in the third row of a standard keyboard are QWERTY.

RAM: Random access memory.

Random access memory: This is the read-write memory available for use in the computer. Through random access the computer can retrieve or send information instantly at any memory address. See memory.

Read: The act of taking data from a storage device, such as a diskette, and putting it in the computer's memory.

Read only memory: A random access memory device that contains permanently stored information. The contents of this memory are set during manufacture. A game cartridge is an example of read only memory.

Read/write memory: Computer memory that you can put data into or take data out of at any time.

Record: An organized block of data. For instance, the payroll information on one person.

Resolution: The number of points (or pixels) you can put on a television screen (or monitor) both vertically and horizontally. High resolution indicates a large number of pixels and, therefore, a sharper display.

Reverse video: Inverse video.

ROM: Read only memory.

SAVE: A command that tells the computer to store the contents of memory on some media, such as a diskette or cassette.

Screen: A CRT or television screen.

Semiconductor: A metal or other material (silicon, for example) with properties between those of conductors and insulators. Its electrical resistance can be changed by electricity, light, or heat.

Serial: A group of events that happen one at a time in sequence. For instance, a serial interface reads in a byte one bit at a time. Modems transmit data serially.

Silicon: A nonmetallic chemical element resembling carbon. It is used in the manufacture of transistors and solar cells.

Slot: See expansion slot.

Software: The programs and data used to control a computer. Software is available in many forms. You can type the program in yourself, or you can have it transmitted to you over the telephone. You can also get it on cassette, diskette, or cartridge.

System: All of the various hardware components that make the computer usable, that is, the computer, printer, modem, keyboard, CRT, and disk drive or cassette player.

Text editor: A computer program that allows you to change or modify the contents of memory. It can modify either data or programs.

Turtle graphics: A small triangular shape that is displayed on the screen when the language Logo is used. The *turtle* shows the direction of lines for graphics. For example, if the instruction is to move north, the turtle moves toward the top of the screen.

User-friendly: A computer system or software package that is easy for novice users to learn.

User's manual: A book or notebook that describes how to use a particular piece of equipment or software.

Variable: A quantity that can assume any of a given set of values. For instance, assume A is a variable whose value is 1. If you add 3 to it, its value becomes 4.

Video display: The screen of your monitor or TV.

Volatile memory: As used with computers, volatile means that the memory loses its contents when the computer is turned off. That is, any information in volatile memory is lost when the computer is turned off.

Window: A portion of the CRT display devoted to a specific purpose.

Word: A minimum storage element in computer memory and the smallest data element worked on by the CPU. Word sizes vary with the design of the computer, varying from eight bits to 12, 16, 32, or 64 bits.

Word processing: A special feature of a computer that allows you to manipulate text. See also word processor or text editor.

Word processor: A computer program that helps you manipulate text. You can write a document, insert or change words, paragraphs, or pages, and then print the document letter-perfect.

Write: To store data on external media such as a disk or cassette. The expression *write to diskette* means that the information stored in the computer's memory is sent to the diskette where it is stored.

Write protect: When new material is written to a diskette, any old material there is erased. Write protect is a method of fixing the disk so that it can't be written on.

Software Publishers

Abacus Associates
6565 W. Loop So.
Suite #220
Bellaire, Texas 77401
(713) 666-8146

Academic Hallmarks
P.O. Box 998
Durango, Colorado 81301
(303) 247-8738

Addison Wesley Publishing Co., Inc.
Jacob Way
Reading, Massachusetts 01867
(617) 944-3700

Adventure International
P.O. Box 3435
Longwood, Florida 32750
(800) 327-7172

ARTSCI, Inc.
5547 Satsuma Avenue
North Hollywood, California 91601
(213) 985-5763

Ashton Tate
10150 W. Jefferson Blvd.
Culver City, California 90230
(213) 204-5570

Apple Computer
10260 Bradley Drive
Cupertino, California 95014
(408) 996-1010

Avalon Hill
Dept. C-10
4517 Harford Road
Baltimore, Maryland 21214
(800) 638-9292

Avant-Garde Creations, Inc.
P.O. Box 30160
Eugene, Oregon 97403
(503) 345-3043

Broderbund Software
17 Paul Drive
San Rafael, California 94903
(415) 456-6424

BudgeCo
428 Pala Avenue
Piedmont, California 94611
(415) 658-8141

Cdex Corporation
5050 El Camino Real
Suite 200
Los Altos, California 94022
(415) 964-7600

CompuServe
5000 Arlington Centre Boulevard
Columbus, Ohio 43220
(614) 457-8600 Headquarters
(614) 224-3113 Branch Office

Computer Advanced Ideas
1442 A Walnut Street, Suite 341
Berkeley, California 94709
(415) 526-9100

Computer Music Journal, The
MIT Press Journals
28 Carlton St.
Cambridge, Massachusetts 02142
(617) 253-2889

Computer Tax Service
P.O. Box 7915
Incline Village, Nevada 89450
(702) 832-1001

Datamost
8943 Fulbright Avenue
Chatsworth, California 91311
(213) 709-1202

Digital Marketing
2363 Blvd. Circle
Walnut Creek, California 94595
(415) 947-1000

DLM, Inc. (Developmental Learning Materials)
One DLM Park
P.O. Box 4000
Allen, Texas 75002
(214) 248-6300

dilithium Press
8285 S.W. Nimbus
Suite 151
Beaverton, Oregon 97005
(800) 547-1842
(503) 646-2713

Dynacomp, Inc.
1427 Monroe Avenue
Rochester, New York 14618
(716) 442-8960

Einstein Corporation
11340 West Olympic Boulevard
Los Angeles, California 90064
(213) 477-4539

Epyx
1043 Kiel Court
Sunnyvale, California 94089
(408) 745-0700

Garbo Software
211 West Fiesta #25
Carlsbad, New Mexico 88220

Harper & Row Publishers, Inc.
10 E. 53 St.
New York, New York 10022
(212) 207-7000

Hayden Book Company
50 Essex St.
Rochelle Park, New Jersey 07662
(201) 368-2202

Houston Instruments
8500 Cameron Rd.
Austin, Texas 78753
(512) 835-0900

Howard W. Sams & Co., Inc.
4300 W. 62nd St.
Indianapolis, Indiana 46268
(317) 298-5400

Huntington Computing
P.O. Box 787
Corcoran, California 93212
(209) 992-5411

Infocom, Inc.
55 Wheeler St.
Cambridge, Massachusetts 02138
(617) 492-1031

InfoWorld Magazine
530 Lytton
Palo Alto, California 94301
(415) 328-4602

Insoft
P.O. Box 19208
Portland, Oregon 97219
(503) 641-5223

Interface Age
McPheters, Wolfe & Jones
16704 Marguardt Ave.
Cerritos, California 90701

J. Fiske Software Systems, Inc.
One University Place
New York, New York 10003

Krell Software Corporation
1320 Stony Brook Rd.
Stony Brook, New York
11790
(516) 751-5139

LAST
619 Sarver Ave.
Montgomery, Alabama 36109
(205) 271-1531

Learning Company, The
4370 Alpine Road
Portola Valley, California
94025
(415) 328-5410

LJK Enterprises
7852 Big Bend Blvd.
St. Louis, Missouri 63119
(314) 962-1855

Micro School Programs
Bertamax, Inc.
3647 Stone Way North
Seattle, Washington 98103
(206) 547-4056

...oft Corporation
...orthrup Way

...ashington 98004
...38

Mind Systems Corporation
P.O. Box 506
Northampton, Massachusetts
01061
(413) 586-6463

Monument Computer Service
P.O. Box 603
Joshua Tree, California 92252
(800) 854-0561

Navic Corporation
P.O. Box 14727
North Palm Beach, Florida
33408
(305) 627-4132

NIBBLE
P.O. Box 325
Lincoln, Massachusetts 01773
(617) 259-9710

NODVILL Software
24 Nod Road
Ridgefield, Connecticut 06877
(203) 431-6449

Odesta
930 Pitner Avenue
Evanston, Illinois 60202
(312) 328-7101

Padware Limited
P.O. Box 14856
Chicago, Illinois 60614
(312) 248-5004

Penguin Software
830 4th Avenue
Geneva, Illinois 60134
(312) 232-1984

Peripherals Plus
39 E. Hanover Avenue
Morris Plains, New Jersey 07950
(800) 631-8112

Personal Computing
Hayden Publishing Company, Inc.
50 Essex St.
Rochelle Park, New Jersey 07662

Phoenix Software, Inc.
64 Lake Zurich Drive
Lake Zurich, Illinois 60047
(312) 438-4850

Popular Computing
McGraw-Hill, Inc.
70 Main St.
Peterborough,
New Hampshire 03458
(603) 924-9281

Proforma Software
2706 Harbor Blvd.
Suite 200
Costa Mesa, California 92626
(714) 641-3846

Quality Software
6660 Reseda Blvd.
Suite 105
Reseda, California 91335
(213) 344-6599

Ritam Corp.
P.O. Box 921
Fairfield, Iowa 52556
(515) 472-8262

Scribner Book Companies, Inc.
597 Fifth Ave.
New York, New York 10017
(212) 486-2700

Sirius Software, Inc.
10364 Rockingham Dr.
Sacramento, California 95827
(916) 366-1195

Sir-Tech Software
6 Main Street
Ogdensburg, New York 13669
(315) 393-6633

Soft Images
200 Route 17
Mahwah, New Jersey 07430
(201) 529-1440

Solutions, Inc.
P.O. Box 989
Montpelier, Vermont 056
(802) 229-0368

Penguin Software
830 4th Avenue
Geneva, Illinois 60134
(312) 232-1984

Peripherals Plus
39 E. Hanover Avenue
Morris Plains, New Jersey 07950
(800) 631-8112

Personal Computing
Hayden Publishing Company, Inc.
50 Essex St.
Rochelle Park, New Jersey 07662

Phoenix Software, Inc.
64 Lake Zurich Drive
Lake Zurich, Illinois 60047
(312) 438-4850

Popular Computing
McGraw-Hill, Inc.
70 Main St.
Peterborough, New Hampshire 03458
(603) 924-9281

Proforma Software
2706 Harbor Blvd.
Suite 200
Costa Mesa, California 92626
(714) 641-3846

Quality Software
6660 Reseda Blvd.
Suite 105
Reseda, California 91335
(213) 344-6599

Ritam Corp.
P.O. Box 921
Fairfield, Iowa 52556
(515) 472-8262

Scribner Book Companies, Inc.
597 Fifth Ave.
New York, New York 10017
(212) 486-2700

Sirius Software, Inc.
10364 Rockingham Dr.
Sacramento, California 95827
(916) 366-1195

Sir-Tech Software
6 Main Street
Ogdensburg, New York 13669
(315) 393-6633

Soft Images
200 Route 17
Mahwah, New Jersey 07430
(201) 529-1440

Solutions, Inc.
P.O. Box 989
Montpelier, Vermont 05602
(802) 229-0368

Krell Software Corporation
1320 Stony Brook Rd.
Stony Brook, New York
11790
(516) 751-5139

LAST
619 Sarver Ave.
Montgomery, Alabama 36109
(205) 271-1531

Learning Company, The
4370 Alpine Road
Portola Valley, California
94025
(415) 328-5410

LJK Enterprises
7852 Big Bend Blvd.
St. Louis, Missouri 63119
(314) 962-1855

Micro School Programs
Bertamax, Inc.
3647 Stone Way North
Seattle, Washington 98103
(206) 547-4056

Microsoft Corporation
10700 Northrup Way
Suite 200
Bellevue, Washington 98004
(206) 828-8088

Mind Systems Corporation
P.O. Box 506
Northampton, Massachusetts
01061
(413) 586-6463

Monument Computer Service
P.O. Box 603
Joshua Tree, California 92252
(800) 854-0561

Navic Corporation
P.O. Box 14727
North Palm Beach, Florida
33408
(305) 627-4132

NIBBLE
P.O. Box 325
Lincoln, Massachusetts 01773
(617) 259-9710

NODVILL Software
24 Nod Road
Ridgefield, Connecticut 06877
(203) 431-6449

Odesta
930 Pitner Avenue
Evanston, Illinois 60202
(312) 328-7101

Padware Limited
P.O. Box 14856
Chicago, Illinois 60614
(312) 248-5004

Source Telecomputing
Corporation
1616 Anderson Road
McLean, Virginia 22102
(703) 821-6660

Sterling Swift Publishing
Company
7901 South IH-35
Austin, Texas 78744
(512) 282-6840

Strategic Simulations, Inc.
883 Stierlen
Building A-200
Mountain View, California
94043
(415) 964-1353

SubLogic Corporation
713 Edgebrook Drive
Champaign, Illinois 61820
(217) 359-8482

Sunburst Communications
Room MM
39 Washington Ave.
Pleasantville, New York
10570
(800) 431-1934

Swearingen Software
6312 West Little York
Suite 197
Houston, Texas 77088

Synergistic Software
830 N. Riverside Drive
Suite 201
Renton, Washington 98055
(206) 226-3216

Toucan Software
4024 Canonero Court
Fair Oaks, California 95628
(916) 966-4241

Versa Computing, Inc.
3541 Old Conejo Road
Suite 104
Newbury Park, California
91320
(805) 498-1956

Virtual Combinatics
P.O. Box 755
Rockport, Massachusetts
01966
(617) 546-6553

VisiCorp
2895 Zanker Rd.
San Jose, California 95134
(408) 946-9000

Wayne Green, Inc.
Instant Software
Elm St.
Peterborough, New Hampshire 03458
(800) 258-5473
(603) 924-9471

Xerox Education Publications
Weekly Reader/Computer
Software Division
Dept. 39-A
245 Long Hill Road
Middleton, Connecticut 06457
(203) 347-7251

Index